Flat Owners' Guide

Fourth Edition

Paul Walentowicz
with Charles Robinson

with a foreword by John Gallagher

Acknowledgements

This book is a new edition of a guide originally published under a different title in 1988. Since the previous edition in 2000, important new rights for flat owners have been introduced by the 2002 Commonhold and Leasehold Reform Act although many of its provisions did not come into force until 2005. These have all been included in this edition. The opportunity has also been taken to improve and update the chapters about service charges, flat management companies and resolving disputes – among others.

No book such as this is possible without the guidance and support of many other people. We would particularly like to thank Naomi Anders, Shelter's Legal and Policy Editorial Manager and Jessica Smith, Shelter's Managing Editor until July 2006. Their contribution helped us enormously. Any errors or omissions remain our responsibility alone.

Paul Walentowicz and Charles Robinson

1st edition: Edmund Jankowski and Perri 6, *Owning Your Flat: A Practical Guide to Problems with your Lease and Landlord*, 1988, London: SHAC (The London Housing Aid Centre).

2nd edition: Paul Walentowicz, *The Flat Owner's Guide*, 1995, London: Shelter.

3rd edition: Paul Walentowicz, *Flat Owners Guide*, 2000, London: Shelter.

ISBN   978 1 903595 18 3

Printed by: Antony Rowe, Wiltshire UK

Typset and published by:
Shelter
88 Old Street
London
EC1V 9HU

0845 458 4590

Registered Company 1038133
Registered Charity 263710

Contents

Foreword

Owning a flat is something of a rollercoaster ride. The new flat owner, having spent far more money than they have ever spent before, is entitled to sink back into their new sofa and contemplate life in their new home. They have exchanged a life of renting, for one of mortgage repayments, and now have accommodation which belongs to them (with a nod to their mortgage lender). They are no longer dependent on their landlord for permission to do basic things such as redecorate or hang pictures, and they are no longer subject to regular increases in rent. They have a home which, in the normal course, is also an appreciating asset.

And yet, much is strangely reminiscent of their previous life in rented accommodation. In most cases, they still have a landlord, usually the freeholder of the block or building containing their flat. The terminology of 'landlord' and 'lessee' seems alien to the concept of owning one's own home, but the new flat owner will usually have signed a lease for a fixed period of time. That period is likely to be 99 or 125 years, well beyond the span of their lifetimes, but the fact remains that their interest is limited in time, and that at some point the flat is destined to revert back to the freeholder. Their lease contains a barrage of obligations and restrictions on their part, and relatively few duties on the part of the landlord. Crucially, the landlord retains the responsibility to maintain the fabric of the building, and to spread the cost of doing so among the leaseholders. The landlord is entitled to apply to the court for forfeiture of the lease if the leaseholder breaches one of the conditions (subject to certain safeguards in favour of the leaseholder). These tribulations are peculiar to the owners of flats: house owners are not troubled by such spectres.

Yet this is too gloomy a picture. Many people live in well-managed developments or converted buildings, and, apart from occasional complaints over the level of this year's service charge contributions, their experience of owning a flat is a largely positive one. Some will spend the rest of their lives in the flat they have purchased. But undeniably there are pitfalls. Partly this is the result of situations where the responsibility for the upkeep of a building lies not with the owner-occupiers of the individual flats, but with a person or company which has the freehold interest, and whose motivation is likely to be commercial. (This will not always be the case: the freeholder may be an individual who actually lives in the building, or it may be a local authority or housing association.) But even where the freeholder is the collective of the flat owners themselves – a flat management company, or a commonhold association – and decisions are taken democratically, there will inevitably be disagreements from time to time between the flat owners, and this may lead to disputes which undermine the effective management of a building for long periods.

The law of flat ownership is based on common law principles of land law and the law of contract, overlaid by statutory controls and by new statutory rights. Over the years, Parliament has recognised that the common law was a patently inadequate tool in seeking to balance the interests of freeholder and leaseholder, or in dealing with issues arising from poor management. It has sought to resolve these problems in various ways. These include: imposing requirements of reasonableness on service charges (Landlord and Tenant Act 1985); giving flat owners a collective right of first refusal where the landlord intends to sell its interest and the right to apply to the court to appoint a manager (Landlord and Tenant Act 1987); creating a right to purchase the freehold collectively in certain circumstances or to extend individual leases (Leasehold Reform, Housing and Urban Development Act 1993); and, most recently, establishing a collective right to manage (Commonhold and Leasehold Reform Act 2002).

In most cases, problems can and should be settled without requiring the intervention of the courts. The issue may be one which falls within the jurisdiction of the Leasehold Valuation Tribunal, in which case the individual flat owner or residents' association may feel able to represent themselves before the Tribunal. If it does become necessary for a flat owner, or a flat management company, to obtain legal representation, this guide will provide the reader with the informed knowledge to enable him or her to make the best use of solicitors.

This is the fourth edition of the Flat Owners' Guide, which has proved an invaluable resource for owners and advisers looking for a path through the maze of legal rules and remedies under the law of England and Wales. Paul Walentowicz, with Charles Robinson, has once again produced a lucid and comprehensive guide. The book has been fully updated to include the impact of the Commonhold and Leasehold Reform Act 2002, notably in introducing the new system of tenure known as commonhold. While not a legal textbook, the guide's strength is that it does not gloss over the complexities of the legislation, but seeks to explain people's rights and obligations in a clear and accessible way. From that foundation, the book addresses problems that can arise and offers practical advice in dealing with them.

This guide will have met its objectives if it assists flat owners to ensure that their buildings are managed fairly and competently; and if it facilitates the resolution of any issues that they encounter, whether by constructive negotiation, or by using external remedies. It should enable flat owners to sleep soundly in the knowledge that there is no problem that is not capable of solution.

John Gallagher
Principal Solicitor
Shelter

Introduction

This new edition of the Flat Owners' Guide includes changes to the legislative framework, to policy and to practice, since the last edition was published in 2000. The authors and the publisher remain committed to advising, helping and informing the owners of flats about the legal, technical and practical issues they face. Flat owners everywhere expect a quality service at a sensible cost. But the reality is often different. Extortionate service charges, neglected maintenance, overlooked repairs and incompetent management are all too frequent. Added to this is a lack of accurate and digestible information from landlords and managing agents.

The labyrinthine nature of the law affecting flat ownership does not help. Disputes between owners, landlords, managing agents and neighbours can bring problems that few people can handle with ease. The guide aims to help flat owners with these and similar matters. Hopefully it will continue to meet their need for clear advice on the wide range of issues they might encounter.

Over recent years, flat ownership has become much more common. In many areas prices have grown to such a level that many people, especially first time buyers, can only afford to buy a flat. In London in particular, there is a shortage of moderately sized and priced houses suitable for the smaller modern household; while on the other hand, there is a large stock of older, bigger properties suitable for conversion into flats. Furthermore, in London and a few other big cities, there is still a residue of large, old blocks of flats, many of which are now sold rather than let. In many inner urban areas, and in many parts of the South and South East of England, property prices are so high or space is so tight, that builders can only profitably erect flats on their new developments. Increasingly too in these areas, developers are converting buildings originally intended as offices into blocks of flats. Local authorities and property developers are under huge pressure to provide an ever-greater number of more affordable homes in high-density developments – which often means flats rather than houses. In addition, there is now a sizeable number of households occupying flats, most often purchased under the Right to Buy legislation, which are in blocks owned by local authorities or other social landlords.

Flat statistics

Just over one million households – 7 per cent of all owners – own a leasehold flat in England. About half (45 per cent) of these privately owned flats are in London. Flats are so common in the London area that almost 28 per cent of all owner-occupied homes in the city are flats. The region with the next highest proportion of flats is the South East, with 9 per cent. They are least common in the East Midlands – 1 per cent of all homeowners – and in Yorkshire and Humberside – 2 per cent of all homeowners. Overall, 80 per cent of leasehold flats are concentrated in the South of England. Almost three-quarters of leasehold flats are in purpose built blocks.

Source: CLG, Survey of English Housing

Many people who are buying, or have bought a flat, simply regard themselves as homeowners, just like their neighbours and friends who live in houses. But in fact, and as regards the law, they are actually tenants with long residential leases. They do, of course, have more rights and obligations than tenants with short leases. In effect, flat owners purchase the temporary ownership of the flat subject to a diverse range of conditions and responsibilities. The landlord retains many rights and responsibilities – such as the duty to repair – over the building or block in which the flat is situated.

Leasehold flats

Leasehold tenure is essentially a phenomenon found only
in England and Wales. In virtually every other country in the
world, including Scotland, you either buy a property, or you
rent a property. Most flats in England and Wales are sold
leasehold because the law made it virtually impossible –
and fraught with complexity – to try to create a freehold
interest of only part of a building. As a result, it is very rare
to come across a flat which is owned freehold. With the
introduction of a new form of freehold tenure –
commonhold – this will gradually change.

Leasehold is a property right held by a tenant (lessee) from the
landlord (lessor) for a specified period on payment of a rent or
lump sum. The entire property reverts to the landlord at the end of
that period. It has its roots far in the past and was originally often
used as security on a loan of money. Although the common law
developed ways to give leaseholders some protection, it was until
very recently heavily weighted in favour of the landlord. Landlords
hold all the 'trump cards' and can often wield an unfair amount of
power over flat owners. They decide spending on maintenance
and repairs; insurance; the upkeep and cleaning of common
areas; the terms of the lease; the service charge and ground rent.

Numerous unscrupulous landlords and property management
companies have made excessive demands on flat owners,
while others neglected or ignored their responsibilities. In some
extreme cases, flat owners have lost their home while still being
required to pay the mortgage debt on the property. Because
of this, it has long been acknowledged that leasehold, while
satisfactory for some, has many drawbacks for long-term
residential leaseholders.

There have been many attempts over the years to try and
reform the laws surrounding leasehold, but these have been

piecemeal and have not always proved to be satisfactory. The latest – and hopefully fruitful – venture at reform came in the 2002 Commonhold and Leasehold Reform Act, which added new and modified existing legislation to that introduced in several other Acts of Parliament. These were the 1985 and 1987 Landlord and Tenant Acts; the 1993 Leasehold Reform, Housing and Urban Development Act; and the 1996 Housing Act. Taken together, these Acts added greatly to the rights of flat owners. Two others, the 1988 Housing Act and the 1989 Local Government and Housing Act introduced changes which, on balance, favoured landlords. Such frequent changes in the law can be difficult to follow and grasp. And as with much new law, it can be hard to explain accurately and definitively how it will work in practice, and how the courts might interpret it.

Summary of a flat owner's main rights

- To buy the freehold of their building
- To take over the management of their building
- To extend their lease
- To buy their landlord's interest in their building if the landlord wants to sell
- To have their building managed properly
- To pay a service charge that is reasonable
- To be consulted about major works

The basis of the landlord and flat owner relationship is the lease. Leases are complex documents that state precisely – although in legal jargon – the terms upon which the sale of the flat is made. These terms are binding on both the landlord and flat owner. In addition to the lease, further rights and responsibilities affecting the landlord and flat owner are found in legislation passed by Parliament, and in case law derived from decisions by the courts.

Like all human relationships, that between flat owner and landlord can go wrong. Not all landlords are good landlords. Some are difficult to contact; others cannot be found at all, some fail to carry out their repairing and other responsibilities; and others overcharge for services. There are frequent disputes about the upkeep and cleaning of blocks of flats and the cost of repairs. Abuses by landlords and their agents remain widespread. Most frequent are complaints about major repairs, service charges, management standards and the competency of managing agents.

In the mid-1980s, an official enquiry highlighted the poor quality of management in many large blocks of flats, including a failure to repair, to collect service charges and to have adequate insurance. This enquiry was instrumental in leading to changes in the law in the 1987 Landlord and Tenant Act, although the impact of those changes was later found to be marginal. Older or larger blocks and conversions tended to have greater problems.

In the early 1990s, a study which concentrated on smaller blocks and conversions found that major problems still existed; the main ones being mismanagement and badly worded leases. Further research in the 1990s confirmed that the 1987 Act had had a limited impact; and was sceptical about the benefits of the 1993 Act, particularly for those living in blocks in a poor state of repair with significant management problems.

Even if a landlord is conscientious and reliable, problems can still arise if, for example, there are technical defects in the lease or the managing agent employed by the landlord does not carry out their duties in a professional manner. Additional problems are created for flat owners, such as a difficulty in selling their property, when their lease only has a short time left to run.

The 2002 Commonhold and Leasehold Reform Act

Despite all the legislative reforms that were made during the 1980s and into the 1990s, many experts believed that the leasehold system remained inherently unjust and unsatisfactory. Although much of the protection looked good on paper, some of the reforms did not – for a number of reasons – work as well as was expected. Despite all the safeguards, devious landlords found ways to continue with old abuses while inventing some new ones. Flat owners found some of the remedies cumbersome, difficult and expensive to use. There were also many inconsistencies, anomalies and gaps in the law, as a result of 30 years of piecemeal – and often rushed – legislation.

The leasehold system remained fundamentally flawed with abuses continuing to flourish, causing misery and distress to thousands of flat owners. Largely this was because the balance of power still remained heavily weighted in favour of landlords at the expense of flat owners. But it was also widely recognised that it would be impossible to abolish the system outright.

Recognising these concerns, in 1998, the Government published a consultation paper proposing further leasehold reform and the introduction of a new system of flat ownership known as 'commonhold'. A further consultation paper, accompanied by a draft Commonhold and Leasehold Reform Bill (published in August 2000), elaborated on the earlier proposals. The commonhold proposals were intended to provide a better system for the future ownership and management of blocks of flats. The Bill received the Royal Assent in 2002.

In summary, the Commonhold and Leasehold Reform Act simplified and extended flat owners' rights in a number of areas, and introduced important changes to the law on service charges. Its key changes concerning leasehold were:

- Introduced the 'Right to Manage' – a right for flat owners to take over the management of their building from the landlord.
- Improved flat owners' rights in relation to service charges and consultation.
- Simplified the purchase of freeholds and lease renewals.
- Introduced restrictions on the start of forfeiture proceedings.
- Extended the jurisdiction of Leasehold Valuation Tribunals in relation to service charges and variation of leases.

Commonhold

The 2002 Act also introduced 'commonhold', a new form of land ownership for blocks of flats as an alternative to leasehold ownership. Under commonhold, occupiers own their flats freehold and, through an association, own and manage the common parts collectively. Commonhold gives flat owners individual ownership of their flats, while having shared ownership of – and shared duties towards – the common parts of the building.

A commonhold consists of individually owned but interdependent freehold properties known as units and common parts. In a block of flats, each flat is a unit and the remainder – including the structure and exterior of the block, the stairs, hallway and grounds – are common parts. Each flat is owned by a unit-holder.

The common parts are owned and managed by a commonhold association, which is a limited company. Only the unit-holders are members of the association. The commonhold is managed by the association, using a commonhold community statement. The statement details the rules of the commonhold, which are partly standard and partly determined by local circumstances. Commonholds must be registered at the Land Registry. Registration applications are usually made by the property developer. Commonhold is available for commercial as well as residential property.

More information about commonhold can be found on the Department for Constitutional Affairs' website (see Chapter 11, Useful publications and Chapter 12, Useful addresses).

The Government hopes commonhold will provide a complete answer to many of the problems that have plagued flat owners over decades. The other reforms have given flat owners brand new rights and enhanced some of their existing ones, for the benefit of those who are not able – or may not wish – to convert to commonhold.

The Act's impact

The Right to Manage offers a practical alternative to flat owners who either do not want, or cannot afford to buy the freehold of their building or block, but who would like to have a greater say in its management. If coupled with a lease extension, it is a cheaper and more attractive option than buying the freehold. Unlike purchasing a freehold, if a Right to Manage company fails, management of the block returns to the landlord. The requirement that a landlord should also be involved as a member of the Right To Manage company seems unnecessary. The exclusion of shared owners – people who have special agreements in which they share ownership of their flat, usually with a housing association – can be criticised on the grounds that they pay 100 per cent of their service charge.

The reforms to service charges were widely welcomed but are complex and far-reaching. The detailed rules are complicated, untested in practice and ambiguous in some respects. The Government's decision in 2005 not to proceed with new rights for flat owners to receive regular statements of their service charges is understandable but regrettable. Following representation by social landlords, the Government considered that this measure would impose considerable extra costs on them; and in turn, on their tenants and flat owners.

The introduction of an alternative to leasehold that gives flat owners full ownership of their homes – the new commonhold tenure – has been generally welcomed. Commonhold flats are freehold: there is no landlord and no lease. Everyone has equal rights. Many of the legal rules that apply to leasehold flats do not apply to commonhold flats. Commonhold community statements are in a standard form and written in clear English, unlike leases that are often hard to understand. This will help to develop common practice and experience across the tenure.

Commonhold is not compulsory. It is unfamiliar and novel to almost everyone involved in the property business. Commonhold is available to the developers of new blocks of flats if they want to use it. If the early schemes are a success, it may become popular. The 2002 Act did not abolish leasehold tenure and it did not include – as might have been expected – any limitation upon the creation of new leaseholds. It is effectively impossible – or at least, extremely difficult – to convert from leasehold to commonhold. This is because the consent of all the current leaseholders and any lenders is required and the leaseholders first need to buy the freehold of the building.

On conversion, the existing freehold owner is not entitled to compensation, so this might prove to be another barrier. So the two systems – one old, one new – will exist side-by-side for many years. There is no obvious commercial benefit in creating a commonhold rather than a leasehold and – in the absence of either prohibition, restriction, tax or other financial incentives – the extent to which commonholds will be used in place of leaseholds is unknown.

But just like self-management by leasehold flat owners, commonhold does require a degree of unanimity and a willingness to co-operate, which can be difficult to achieve in practice. Commonhold does not offer the rights and protections against bad landlords that leasehold provides, and there is no requirement for 'reasonableness' of expenditure as there is under a lease.

Supporters of the 2002 Act believe that the Government had at long last listened to both flat owners and landlords by addressing many of the loopholes and anomalies in the current system. The Leasehold Advisory Service said: 'They have listened to tenants and produced the goods… Where a landlord owns a building, you can't simply wave a magic wand and transfer ownership… The government is not into confiscation, but what they have done is create an alternative system.'

Although most experts, advisers, professional associations and campaigning groups welcomed the changes the 2002 Act brought in, not everyone shared this optimism. Opponents claimed that it simply fiddled about with the failures of the leasehold system. Austin Mitchell, a Labour MP, described the Bill as 'a timorous mouse of a proposal'. He was concerned that leasehold would survive, that current flat owners would effectively be prevented from converting to commonhold and that the new legislation offered nothing to the leasehold owners of houses.

The Campaign for the Abolition of Residential Leaseholds said: 'These measures, like its 80 predecessors in the last century, merely tinkers and fails to give leaseholders the means to win their homes'. The Conservative opposition spokesman claimed that Labour's proposals were nothing more than 'another eye-catching initiative'. Time and experience will be the judge of these different views.

The extension of the jurisdiction of Leasehold Valuation Tribunals was widely approved. But there are doubts whether Tribunal funding is sufficient to enable them to exercise their new powers and keep within a reasonable timescale. Tribunal delays of eight months or more are not uncommon.

The 2002 Act did not tackle the problem of poor managing agents, who remain unregulated, and there is no form of quality assurance to enable landlords or flat management companies to employ agents with confidence. There are far too many incompetent and 'cowboy' agents. There is no scheme to regulate and control managers and managing agents. It must become a regulated profession with a national supervisory body.

Our aims

The aim of this book is to provide a practical guide for flat owners – and their advisers – about their rights and responsibilities in any specific situation; how and when to exercise them; and how to deal with many of the problems they might encounter. It explains:

- The special points to look out for when buying a flat (Chapter 1).
- The long residential leasehold system including your rights:

if you want to vary your lease

when your lease expires and

on 'ground rents' and 'forfeiture' (Chapter 1).

- Your rights on service charges and major works (Chapter 2).
- Your right to take over the management of your building collectively (Chapter 6).
- Your right to buy the freehold of your building collectively (Chapter 3).
- Your right to extend your lease (Chapter 5).
- Your right to buy your landlord's interest in your building collectively if he or she wants to sell (Chapter 4).
- Your rights to information and to be consulted about, for example, insurance and managing agents (Chapter 2).
- Your rights to seek the appointment of a manager for your building, and to compulsorily buy your landlord out (Chapter 6).
- Some of your rights about the permissions that you may need from your landlord, for example, if you want to make alterations to your flat (Chapter 6).
- The practicalities of running a flat management company (Chapter 7).
- The various methods of resolving disputes (Chapter 8).

Leasehold law uses many technical terms and phrases whose meaning is hard or impossible for most lay people, and some professionals, to grasp. A glossary (Chapter 9) explains those which are in most common use and those used in this guide. The guide ends with chapters giving:

- The main Acts of Parliament relevant to flat owners (Chapter 10).
- Useful publications (Chapter 11).
- Useful addresses (Chapter 12).
- The addresses of Leasehold Valuation Tribunals (Chapter 13).

Most of what is said about flats in this guide applies equally to maisonettes. A maisonette is, usually, similar to a self-contained flat with its own separate entrance; but on two floors rather than one, with no shared stairway. Apartments and penthouses are also flats in law.

The law covered in this guide is that applying in England and Wales only. Scotland has its own very different – and in many respects superior – legal arrangements to cater for flat ownership. Leasehold ownership is almost unknown in Scotland, and the great majority of flats are owned on a form of tenure that is analogous to freehold.

The law relating to flats also applies – with some important exceptions – to flat owners whose landlord is not a private individual or company. This includes public or social landlords, such as local authorities and housing associations. Many flat owners occupy former local authority or housing association homes bought under the Right to Buy or similar legislation. Many others have bought a lease from social housing landlords under low-cost home ownership initiatives, leasehold schemes for the elderly, and other schemes. When relevant, these exceptions and exemptions are mentioned in the text.

Leasehold flats formerly in the social housing sector

About 27 per cent of all leasehold flats were formerly in the social sector. Eighty-seven percent of these are in the South of England, with 58 per cent in London. The freehold in 56 per cent of ex-social sector leasehold flats is held by local authorities, which continue, in the main, to provide management services. Many are still owned and occupied by the former tenants of these flats.

Source: CLG, Survey of English Housing

This guide is not aimed – except incidentally – at the owners of leasehold houses, whose right, for example, to buy their freehold or extend their lease is different from that of flat owners. However, leasehold house owners have similar rights to flat owners over, for example, service charges.

Neither is this guide aimed – except incidentally – at most public and private sector tenants who have short-term leases or tenancies (leases of less than 21 years when originally granted). But if such a tenant pays a variable service charge, then similar rules to those covered in Chapter 2 also apply to them. They may also qualify under the Right of First Refusal (see Chapter 4) and in a few other areas.

It should be kept in mind that enforcing your legal rights may mean – and in some circumstances should always mean – hiring a lawyer, and sometimes also going to a tribunal or court. Legal action is usually expensive and often protracted. It is preferable to try to avoid it. It is often sensible to try to settle a disagreement informally, or to use an alternative method of dispute resolution, before contemplating legal action. In many situations, leasehold disputes have to be referred to a tribunal, which, although likely to be less expensive than action in a court, is not necessarily quicker. Reference to a court in the guide is to a County Court in England and Wales, unless otherwise stated.

This guide is not a legal textbook and it is not intended to be a substitute for professional advice, assistance and representation. It is aimed at the intelligent reader who wishes to know more about their rights as a flat owner; the sort of problems or difficulties they might face; and what they can do about them.

While every effort has been made to make the guide as accurate and up-to-date as possible, the authors and publisher are unable to accept responsibility for any errors it may contain. They welcome comments, criticism and suggestions that will be taken account of in a future edition. In addition, they are interested in hearing from anyone with something to say about leasehold flats – their experiences, stories, new ways of tackling old problems, etc.

Flat Owners' Guide: Your rights at a glance

	Private sector landlord	Local authority landlord	Landlord is a charitable housing trust/ association	Landlord is a non-charitable housing trust/ association	Shared owners with less than 100 per cent share	Chapter in this guide
Right to enfranchise	Yes	Yes	No	Yes	No	3
Right of First Refusal	Yes	No	No	No	No	4
Right to renew lease (lease extension)	Yes	Yes	No	Yes	No	5
Right to Manage	Yes	No, but there is a separate scheme	Yes	Yes	No	6
Compulsory appointment of a manager	Yes	No	No	No	No	6
Compulsory acquisition	Yes	No	No	No	No	6
Variation of lease	Yes	Yes	Yes	Yes	Yes	1
Service charge controls	Yes	Yes, mostly	Yes, mostly	Yes	Yes	2

This table is a summary only. Note that exceptions may apply: for example, a resident landlord in a converted building, or 25 per cent non-residential use. Refer to the relevant chapters for information about exceptions.

Leasehold flats

1

Introduction

In England and Wales there are two ways to own land: freehold and leasehold. To be precise, there is now a third – commonhold – the new way of owning interdependent properties such as flats, shops and offices. It is an alternative to long leasehold ownership. Technically though, commonhold is an area of freehold land consisting of units or flats and common parts. (See the Introduction for more information about commonhold).

Freehold and leasehold each have their advantages and disadvantages in specific circumstances. Freehold is close to absolute ownership. Leasehold confers ownership for a temporary period, subject to the terms and conditions contained in the contract or lease. Houses are usually freehold, although there remains a large number of leasehold houses mostly concentrated in the north of England.

Almost all flats are leasehold. Most flat owners are leaseholders or, technically, tenants with a long lease. Somebody else owns the freehold of the property; this may be an individual, a private company or even all the leaseholders collectively. A flat owner may hold their lease direct from the freeholder or from an intermediate leaseholder. In nearly all cases, a flat owner will have a landlord.

A lease is a legally binding contract agreed between a flat owner and their landlord. It sets out the rights and duties of both.

This chapter discusses and explains:

- Buying a flat.
- The leasehold system.
- Varying leases.
- What happens when leases expire.
- Ground rents and 'forfeiture'.

Maisonettes

Two common types of 'maisonette' are found in Britain. One type is a self-contained dwelling forming part of a building with accommodation on two floors; in effect, a two-floor flat. In the United States, they are known as 'duplexes'. This type of maisonette is a flat in law.

The second is a type of building that is familiar in southern England. Externally, it looks like a single house, but the ground and first floors are built to be separately occupied. They do not inter-connect, and each has their own front door at ground level. Each floor is called a 'maisonette'. Such properties have been treated as 'a house' for individual leasehold enfranchisement.

Nevertheless, many of the rights covered in this book – except possibly those relating to collective enfranchisement and the Right of First Refusal – apply equally to this kind of maisonette. Owners of this type of property who are contemplating action of any kind should first seek expert legal advice about their rights in law.

Buying a flat

Buying a flat is similar to buying a house, but some account has to be taken of the fact that you will be sharing the property with other flat owners, and that you will be buying a lease to the flat. These bring a variety of different considerations and added legal complications. What the new owner actually buys from the vendor is the lease, which grants temporary ownership – or a tenancy – of the flat rather than the flat outright. The freehold of the property in which the flat is situated is owned by somebody else.

There may be intermediate leaseholders too. Intermediate leaseholds and freeholds can be bought and sold just as flats can be bought and sold. In fact, some people trade in residential leaseholds and freeholds – usually those of large blocks – as a form of investment.

Apartments and penthouses

In case there is any doubt: an 'apartment' – whether 'luxury' or not – is a flat in law. An apartment is – or was – US English for a flat, and has been imported into Britain in recent years. Developers constructing and agents selling flats rarely, if ever, describe them as flats in brochures and elsewhere nowadays. They are nearly always 'apartments'.

If you are fortunate enough to own a 'penthouse' – meaning a home on the roof or top floor of a tall building – that is a flat in law too.

Your landlord – either the freeholder or an intermediate leaseholder – retains many rights and has many obligations over the premises. Equally, a flat owner has a large and varied number of rights, responsibilities, restrictions and liabilities. These are set out in the lease itself. Typically, a lease will set out who is responsible for looking after different parts of the property and for insuring them. In most cases, a landlord will be responsible for the maintenance, repair and insurance of the fabric of the building, and leaseholders will be obliged to pay a proportion of the costs through service charges.

Leases may also restrict how the property may be used (for example, business activities may be forbidden), or prohibit subletting to some categories of tenant. A lease will usually oblige a flat owner to pay a 'ground rent' and to reimburse the landlord for any expenditure they incur on the building, through a regular 'service charge'. Your lease will allow you to occupy your flat for a fixed number of years: a period that reduces over time from the date when it was originally granted.

Before you buy your flat, you should try to understand what the main terms of the lease are – your solicitor should be able to help.

Typical responsibilities of flat owners are:

- To pay an annual ground rent – usually a small sum; sometimes nothing.

- To pay a share of the costs of looking after and running the building (usually known as a service or maintenance charge).

- To look after their flat and the property as a whole.

- To observe the terms of the lease regarding making alterations to their flat, subletting, behaviour, etc.

Many blocks of flats are collectively owned and/or managed by the flat owners themselves; but most are owned and managed by someone who does not live in the property. You should find out who owns and/or runs the building and – if it is collectively owned and/or managed by the flat owners themselves – decide if you are prepared to contribute to the management yourself. Although attendance at meetings, etc is always voluntary, so is buying a flat in a leaseholder-managed block.

Leaseholder or resident-managed blocks should be looked after better and more economically, while residents only discuss and decide the kinds of issues – say, when to get the exterior painted – an individual house owner would do for themselves anyway. More and more flat owners have decided to own and/or manage their blocks themselves; often by using powers made available to them by Parliament. Sometimes they took this decision because their landlord did not look after the building properly, or ignored other of their responsibilities.

Example

A survey on behalf of a prospective purchaser of a flat in a small block in London found damp in the communal parts of the house and that almost £600 of roof repairs were needed. But the other flat owners said that no repairs had been carried out despite frequent requests. Furthermore, the landlord should have provided buildings cover for the property and paid the premium out of the annual service charge. But this appeared not to have been done. Both the landlord and the managing agent failed to reply to her enquiries.

If you are buying a new flat or a flat that has not been leased before you are entitled, in theory at least, to negotiate any terms that you wish. In practice, however, this can be difficult. There are certain terms that are almost always included in residential leases (see Normal clauses included in long leases, page 39). Furthermore, the vendor may only be prepared to sell the flat to you if you agree to certain terms. As there is usually a shortage of accommodation, people selling flats are generally in a stronger position than people wanting to buy, so the terms of leases tend to favour them. Even so, it is important to try to ensure that the lease gives you the rights you need to live in the flat securely and comfortably. If you do not understand, or are concerned about something, ask your solicitor or conveyancer for advice. Leases, like all legal documents, can contain errors. It can be very difficult for someone to sell their flat if their lease is seriously faulty. But it is possible to get certain defects in a lease remedied (see Varying leases, page 41).

Example

A first-time buyer liked the flat she looked over but it had an extremely high service charge and nobody could explain where all the money was going. Another flat she wanted was at the centre of a long-running dispute over a repair bill of several thousand pounds. The flat owners had had no advance warning about the work being done nor had they been given any estimates.

If you are buying a flat from an existing flat owner, the lease is transferred to you with all its rights and obligations. The transfer or sale of a lease is called an 'assignment'. It is difficult to renegotiate the terms of an existing lease with a landlord, but occasionally this is possible by entering into a further document called a 'Deed of Variation'. If you cannot agree, you may be able to get some of the terms of the lease changed (see Varying leases, page 41) once you have bought the flat.

The different terms used when dealing with flats

Ordinary language	Legal language
Flat owner, owner-occupier, home owner	Tenant, long leaseholder, lessee
Landlord, building owner, property owner, block owner	Landlord, lessor, freeholder
Lease, flat ownership	Lease, tenancy

The preferred terms used in this book are flat owner, landlord and lease

---

Another question on which you should satisfy yourself before purchase is the length of the outstanding term remaining on the lease. Leases on flats are for a fixed number of years; typically 99 or 125 years when granted. You need to know how many years are left to run on the lease. Although a flat with a short outstanding term may be relatively cheap to buy, it may be difficult or impossible to obtain a mortgage on it. People are used to the idea of property constantly appreciating in value. However, at a certain stage – say with less than 30 years left to run – that is not necessarily true of a leasehold flat. And if the remaining term is very short, it may prove impossible to sell at all. The lease will expire automatically at the end of the term, although most leaseholders have a right to stay on as renting tenants at the end of the lease (see What happens when leases expire? page 45). Most flat owners also have the right to buy their freehold (see Chapter 3) or to renew their lease (see Chapter 5).

You should – like any other prospective homebuyer – have a survey of the property carried out by a qualified surveyor. In older blocks, it is advisable to have a full structural survey done – or as full as is possible – and not one of the cheaper alternatives promoted by many mortgage lenders.

Home Information Packs (HIPs)

From June 2007, all homeowners – or their selling agents – will be required to have a Home Information Pack (HIP) when marketing homes for sale, and to make a copy of the pack available to prospective buyers on request. The packs are designed to speed up the home buying process. HIPs will contain information such as the title documents, the lease, warranties and guarantees for any building work and results of local authority searches. A property condition report may be included.

Be aware that many, if not most, estate agents and many professionals involved in the property purchase business often fail to warn people about the problems they may encounter with leasehold flats, most of which are to do with maintenance, service charges and management. Think carefully, for example, if you are tempted to buy a competitively priced flat, typically one in a low-value 1930s purpose-built block or other older converted property. If the price reflects the property's poor condition, you could find yourself in an increasingly shabby building, lacking the financial resources to pay for the necessary renovation work. It may be sensible to upgrade the building, which would be to everyone's benefit, but the flat owners cannot afford to do it.

Another not uncommon scenario is if a landlord also owns a lot of flats in the building, it may not be in his interest to spend a great deal of money on it, because he may plan to buy further properties as they become available. If the building becomes really dilapidated, owners who want to move may find that they have to sell to their landlord because their flats have become too difficult to sell at a fair price on the open market.

Advice before buying a flat

- Check out the appearance and condition of the outside and inside of the block. Look out for any obvious signs of neglect or misuse. For example, peeling paintwork, broken windows, an unkempt garden, a scruffy entrance hall, damaged carpets, etc. The state of the rubbish bin area is often a good indicator.

- Speak to other residents. Find out what relationship they have with the landlord and the managing agent. Ask if there are any disputes or major works outstanding. Find out how quickly problems are resolved. If they are unhappy, they will tell you.

- If the block is owned and/or managed by the residents, speak to the Secretary of the leaseholders' association.

Again, ask if there are any disputes or major works outstanding. Try to find out if they are happy with their managing agent if there is one. Ask about the amounts being spent, why and when.

- Find out if there are any 'rules of the block', and if they are enforced. Availability of information is a good sign. You should also be able to get up-to-date accounts on demand.

- Try to find out how many flats are let to tenants. There is some evidence to suggest that blocks with a high proportion of tenants are less well looked after than those without.

- Try contacting the landlord and managing agent and asking any questions you have about the property. Ask the managing agent how often staff visit the property. Ask the landlord if he owns any of the flats in the block. If they cannot be contacted easily, or are unwilling to answer, this might be time to think again.

- If the freehold is owned by a limited company, it might be worth making a search through Companies House to check the landlord's financial circumstances and if, in fact, the company has filed recent accounts. Landlords with problems are very likely to cause problems for flat owners.

- Be clear how much the service charge is, what it covers and how it is varied. Make sure any money paid by leaseholders is kept under trust in a separate account.

- Ask if the residents have considered exercising any of their rights under legislation allowing them to buy their freehold or take over management of the building.

There is no guarantee that even if you follow all the advice given above, you will never encounter any problems. Even if you do not get satisfactory answers to all your questions, you should have a clearer idea of what to expect. There may be good reasons why you may not be or feel able to ask any of them at all. But at the very minimum, you should try to speak to other residents, to check out the landlord and the managing agent and have a survey done.

The leasehold system

Leasehold ownership of a flat is, in law, a long or a very long tenancy. It gives the right to occupy and have sole use of the flat for a long but fixed period of time – the 'term' of the lease. This is often for 99 or 125 years but it can be as long as 999 years. The flat can be bought and sold many times during the term. The term is set at the beginning of the lease and so decreases over time. If it were not for inflation, the value of the flat would fall over the term until the eventual expiry of the lease. Leasehold flats can be in converted houses or purpose-built blocks and, in either case, above commercial or retail premises.

Flat ownership usually relates to everything within the four external walls of the flat, including floorboards and plaster to the internal walls and ceilings. It does not usually include external or structural walls. The building and the land it is on is owned by someone else, usually the landlord, who is responsible for the maintenance, repair and insurance of the building. The landlord can be the freehold owner or have a lease of the building. The landlord can be a person or a company. Many flat owners own the freehold of the building themselves, through a leaseholders' or residents' management company, effectively becoming their own landlord.

A lease is a private contract between a leaseholder and a landlord. It sets out their respective contractual obligations; what the leaseholder has contracted or promised to do; and what the landlord is obliged or bound to do. In effect, a lease spells out what each party's rights and responsibilities are, although not in clear language. Few flat owners ever read their leases; fewer still understand them. Like most homebuyers faced with complicated-looking documents, such as title deeds or mortgage agreements, flatowners often opt for their solicitor or conveyancer to check their leases over for them. In the case of leases this can be a mistake because, if the truth be told, many professionals do not check them thoroughly enough either, or simply take them for granted. Most residential property bought and sold is freehold not leasehold. There is little pressure on anyone – professional or layperson – to understand either the concept, the principles or the detail of a lease.

Residential leases are undoubtedly heavy going. English law has developed a jargon of legal terms and expressions that are incomprehensible to most people. This is especially true of leases, and of the terms that are included in them. Coming to grips with some of this language is a necessary evil and certain important concepts and principles do need to be grasped. All flat owners should, at the very least, understand what these are. They are:

- The person who creates or grants a lease is known as the lessor or landlord; the person to whom it is granted is the lessee, leaseholder or tenant. A landlord may be the freeholder of the building or may themselves be a leaseholder. In this book the term 'flat owner' is used to describe a lessee, a leaseholder, or a tenant with a long lease who owns, or is buying a flat or maisonette; although this is not a legal term. Flat owners may hold their lease direct from the freeholder, or from an intermediate leaseholder. When this guide refers to 'your landlord' this means – unless otherwise stated – your immediate landlord.

- When a lease is created, the landlord retains the freehold of the property, unless the landlord is also a leaseholder him or herself. This is known as the landlord's 'reversion' because at the end of the lease, the property reverts back to the landlord, subject to certain exceptions. At its simplest, therefore, at any one time there are two owners of the property – the landlord and the flat owner – but each owns a different interest. One owns the freehold, the other the leasehold. If there are intermediate leases, then there can be many more people with an interest in the property. Although there can only be one freehold owner of a building, there can be any number of leases on all or separate parts of it.

Example

Company A owns the freehold of a building with lots of flats. In 1994 it granted a lease of the whole block to Company B for 125 years. In 1995 Company B started to sell individual flats in the building on 99 year leases. In this situation Company A is the 'head' lessor. Company B is the 'head' lessee. Individual flat owners are 'sub or under-lessees'. Company B is the direct or immediate landlord and Company A is the superior landlord of the flat owners. In order to exercise their rights, it is important that flat owners can identify the ownership of the leases and the freehold of their block.

- A landlord can sell the freehold, sell the lease, or grant a new lease on their property, and a flat owner can sell or assign the remaining period of their lease. The effect is that a new landlord or a new flat owner steps into the shoes of the original parties. This can happen any number of times during the term of a lease.

- The rights and duties of a flat owner are governed by their lease, subject to the rights and duties that the freeholder retains, which are also stated in the lease. Leases may compel flat owners to do positive things such as pay a service charge, and allow landlords to do things such as entering the flat to carry out an inspection, or compel them to do other things such as insuring the building containing the flat. Flat owners can do more or less whatever they want in their flats, provided they do not break the terms of their lease. However, if a flat owner breaches any of the terms of their lease, their landlord may have a right to 'forfeit' the lease and attempt to recover possession of the property. But legislation provides a range of measures to protect flat owners. (See 'Ground rents and forfeiture' page 47).

What are leases?

Unlike a freehold which gives the buyer what is, in effect, complete ownership of the land and the building(s) on it forever, a lease confers only a limited ownership of the property for a fixed period of time. Your lease will allow you to occupy your flat for a fixed number of years – known as the 'term'. The lease diminishes from the term that was originally granted, and the outstanding term will depend on what was left when you took over the lease.

Example

A person buys a flat in 2005. The term of the lease was 125 years when originally granted in 1985. The outstanding term is 105 years.

A lease is carved out of the freehold of the landlord and can take a number of forms. At one end of the spectrum there is, for example, the tenancy of a furnished bed-sit, providing short-term accommodation at a weekly rent; at the other is the long-term lease bought for a large capital sum or premium, with only a nominal ground rent payable. The rules are very different depending on whether someone occupies their home on a short-term or a long-term basis. Broadly speaking, people with a long-term tenancy have greater rights.

This book is primarily aimed at flat owners with a long (term) lease or tenancy on their home – however long there remains to run on it – and not at tenants who have short leases or tenancies, except incidentally. In law, many maisonettes are flats, so this book also applies to people who own, or are buying, a maisonette. So too are apartments and penthouses.

For a tenancy to arise, several conditions must be met:

- There must be a landlord and a tenant.
- There must be 'exclusive possession' which is, essentially, the right to occupy the premises to the exclusion of all others, including the landlord.
- There must be identifiable land.
- The grant must be for a definite period.
- The landlord must retain a 'reversion', the right to get possession when the tenancy expires, but this may subsequently be sold.

To qualify as a 'long' tenancy, three further conditions must be satisfied:

- A long tenancy is a tenancy originally granted for a term exceeding 21 years, whether or not it has been subsequently extended. Typical terms for a long tenancy are 99, 125 or 999 years.
- It must be at a low rent. If the tenancy was entered into before 1 April 1990, the rent payable must be less than two-thirds of the rateable value of the property. If the tenancy was entered into on or after that date, the rent payable must be:

  £1,000 or less a year if the property is in Greater London, or

  £250 or less a year if the property is elsewhere.
- It must satisfy the 'qualifying condition'. In simple terms, this means that it is excluded from Rent or Housing Act protection.

In most situations there is no doubt that a flat owner has a valid long lease. The lease is an important document and you should make sure that you obtain and keep a copy. It sets out the rights and duties of the landlord and the leaseholder. It will normally define who is responsible for looking after the different parts of the building and for insuring it. It may also restrict how the property may be used (for example, business activities may be banned). The lease will usually require flat owners to reimburse the landlord for any expenditure they make on the building, through a regular service charge (see Normal terms included in long leases, page 39).

Ground rents

The low or 'ground rent' payable under a long residential lease is often a modest sum; perhaps £50 or £100 a year. The precise amount, or some method of calculating it, will be stated in the lease. Since ground rents are normally insignificant, the question arises as to why they are there at all. There are two reasons.

The first is that an annual payment constitutes a 'consideration' in law without which there can be no valid contract; and a lease is, after all, a rather detailed contract. It is called a 'rent' because leasehold is a tenancy. There are examples of ground rents that just comply with this criterion. Typically, they are known as 'peppercorn rents': in other words a flat owner has nothing to pay at all. In this case, the lease does not specify an amount of ground rent.

The second reason is because such a relatively small sum is unlikely to affect the sale price; many landlords take the view that as long as it is not actually more bother than it is worth, they may as well collect it.

Although a ground rent is usually a nominal amount, it is important that it is paid promptly. Many leases allow a landlord to commence court proceedings to bring the lease to an end if the rent is in arrears (see Ground rents and forfeiture, page 47). A problem related to the fact that a ground rent is usually a modest amount is that some landlords do not bother to demand or collect it at all (again, see Ground rents and forfeiture, page 47).

Some landlords have introduced ground rents set at an initial figure, which is not altogether nominal, and which rise over intervals. They may rise to a predetermined amount, or they may be subject to a review based on a percentage of capital or rental value. But the ground rent must not be variable within 20 years of the grant of the lease, or more frequently than at intervals of 21 years afterwards. Ground rents on long leases are limited by the low rent condition discussed earlier. If a ground rent is above the relevant amount, the tenancy will not be a long tenancy in law, with the consequence that a flat owner would not have most of the rights that they might expect. This is another reason why you should check out a lease before you buy a flat.

Landlords and flat owners are bound by all of the terms of a lease unless both agree to change any of them. In some circumstances, certain terms of a lease may be changed in the absence of agreement (see Varying leases, page 41). If the lease states that either the landlord or the flat owner must do something, then they must do so.

If one party breaks a term of the lease, then the other party can take action. For example, if the lease states that the landlord must repair a specific part of the property and this is not done, then the flat owner can get a court to order the landlord to do the repairs and, perhaps, pay compensation (see Chapter 6). On the other hand, one party may go to court to get an order that the other party stop doing something (for example, running a business from their flat) which is prohibited by the lease. Generally, landlords and flat owners are not obliged to do particular things unless there is a specific clause in the lease stating that they must do so. There are, however, some exceptions.

Some of the clauses in the lease may be overridden by an Act of Parliament. For example, the obligation of a flat owner to pay a particular amount of service charge may be overridden by the provisions of the 1985 Landlord and Tenant Act as amended (see Chapter 2). Similarly, the common law right of a landlord to evict a flat owner for breaking a clause of the lease (the legal phrase is 'to re-enter' and 'forfeit' the lease) is limited by the provisions of the 1977 Protection from Eviction Act as amended, and by other statutory protection for leaseholders (see Ground rents and forfeiture, page 47).

Leasehold flats and the public sector

Some of the rights flat owners have do not apply to the owners of properties held on leases from public sector bodies and some charities. (See the table following the Introduction on page 21).

There may be some rights read into a lease even though they are not specifically spelt out in it. A right or an obligation that is read into a lease in this way is known as an 'implied' right or obligation. Some of these implied rights are called 'easements'. An easement is a right that a property owner is entitled to exercise over other property (for example, a right of way). Generally, rights are only read into leases if they are both absolutely necessary to make the contract work and, in all the circumstances, reasonable. For example, if a flat owner would not be able to live normally in the flat if these rights were not included; or if they were so obvious that everyone would have included them in the lease if they had thought about them at the time the lease was granted. Some well-established implied rights or obligations include:

- The right to support: a landlord cannot demolish or neglect the lower floors if this would mean that an owner's flat on an upper floor would collapse.

- Access through the hall, lift, stairs, drives and entrance: a landlord cannot do anything which stops or makes it substantially more difficult for the flat owner to get into their flat.

- The right to the continuation of existing services: a landlord cannot do anything which leads to the disconnection or termination of existing services such as gas, water, electricity, telephone, postal delivery, etc. This does not apply to personal services such as caretaking. If a caretaker is to be provided, there should be a specific clause to that effect in the lease.

- Repair and upkeep of common parts: in some cases there may be an implied obligation that a landlord maintains stairs, lifts, lighting in halls, rubbish chutes, etc.
- A landlord also has an implied duty to ensure that people using the common parts are reasonably safe from injury arising from defects to the building. In general, a landlord will be able to pass on the costs of this obligation in service charges (see Chapter 2).

There is no right to privacy read into a lease. However, a landlord only has a right to come into a flat in accordance with specific terms set out in a lease.

Normal terms included in long leases

There is not enough space to give a complete catalogue of all the terms or conditions contained in leases. The following list contains some of the more important that are normally included:

- Description of the property: the flat may be described simply in words, or in words together with a plan. It is obviously important that this is done precisely so that it is clear what the resident owns. Most leases state who is responsible for the walls, ceilings and floors of a flat.
- The price paid by the original flat owner, the ground rent payable and how the service charge is calculated.

Service charges

A service charge is the payment by a flat owner to their landlord for all the services the landlord provides. The lease will explain how it is calculated and apportioned between the flat owners. It will also detail what can and cannot be charged by the landlord. Service charges normally vary. They can go up or down without limit, provided they are reasonable. Flat owners have rights to challenge unreasonable service charges (see Chapter 2).

- The length of the lease when it was originally granted and the date when it was granted.
- The services which the landlord is obliged to provide (for example, caretaking, cleaning and lighting of the common parts).
- Some leases allow the landlord to create a 'reserve fund'.

Reserve funds

Many leases allow landlords to collect money in advance to build up a 'reserve' or 'sinking' fund. This is to make sure that sufficient funds are available for future scheduled important work. Payment is normally included in the service charge. (See Chapter 2).

- Details about other parts of the building the flat owner is allowed to use (for example, halls, car parking spaces, garden).
- Details of who else is allowed access to the flat (for example, neighbouring flat owners if this is necessary to carry out repairs to their flat, landlord's surveyor).
- Repairing and redecorating obligations: leases usually make flat owners responsible for repairs and decorations to their flat and sometimes for the external walls of the flat. The landlord should always be responsible for repairs to those parts of the building which are not leased.
- A clause allowing the landlord to 're-enter' the flat if the flat owner breaks any of the obligations contained in the lease (see Ground rents and forfeiture, page 47).

- Clauses relating to the use of the flat (for example, forbidding business activities, not to make structural alterations without permission, provisions about subletting).

- A clause forbidding leaseholders to cause a nuisance, annoyance or disturbance.

- Insurance: there should be an obligation on someone to keep the whole building insured. This is usually the landlord.

- A clause that other owners or occupiers in the building will have to observe similar clauses in their leases, and that other leases in the building will contain similar clauses.

Useful Hints

- Make sure you understand as clearly as possible the main terms of your lease before you buy your flat.

- Keep a copy of your lease.

- When you get a copy of your lease, read through each clause and write a short summary of each, in plain English, in the margin of a spare copy of the lease.

- Ask your solicitor or someone with expert knowledge to explain anything in the lease you do not understand.

Varying leases

Leases can often be defective in a number of ways. They may not make provision for the insurance of the building. They may be ambiguous or badly drafted. Such defects can make the proper management of the property very difficult. Such defects – or any other of a lease's provisions – can be corrected or varied at any time with the mutual agreement of the parties concerned. Leases may also need to be altered because of a change of circumstances as the next example shows.

Example

A building contained ten flats. Each flat owner paid a proportion of the total service charge. The building was split into two parts and one part was sold. As a result, the proportion of the service charge paid by the remaining flat owners needed to be recalculated. Their leases had to be amended. The flat owners and the landlord all agreed.

But agreement may not always be possible. Experience suggests that if there are more than a few flats in a building, the likelihood of getting the consent of all the flat owners is low. Landlords may refuse to give their approval to the variation of one or more leases. Even if all those involved do agree, it is usually also necessary to obtain the approval of any mortgage lenders with an interest in the property. The process will often be expensive because flat owners will normally be expected to pay all of the costs involved in having a lease or leases varied.

Example

'Unfortunately, in our lease it does say we should have Reserves, but it says "after consultation" ... Now what on earth does that mean? Because all (the managing agents do) is produce these large documents to us and they say, "We'd like to talk to you about this, and this is what we're going to do"... fait accompli, and it's done, we can't argue about it'.

Resident, large converted block in Berkshire

If agreement between the parties is not possible, the 1987 Landlord and Tenant Act gave flat owners and landlords the right to ask a court to make an order varying a lease in certain circumstances. The process of applying to a court can be lengthy and costly, particularly because an unsuccessful flat owner may be liable for their landlord's costs. Recognising this, the 2002 Commonhold and Leasehold Reform Act transferred jurisdiction from the courts to Leasehold Valuation Tribunals (LVTs). A lease can be varied if it fails to make satisfactory provision for certain management-related matters. These are:

- The repair or maintenance of the flat, the block, or any land or building which is leased to the flat owner and any installations or services. For example, a LVT could change the lease to require a landlord to keep the structure of the block, including the roof, walls and foundations, in repair, if the lease did not require this. Or the lease could be varied to ensure that a landlord has to maintain a block's hot water and heating system.

- The insurance of the property: A lease could be varied to compel a landlord to insure the building (see Insurance, page 122).

- The calculation of service charges: A lease could be altered to ensure that a landlord cannot recover from the flat owners in service charges more than has been spent on the building, including management or administration charges. A lease might also be altered to ensure that service charges are fairly calculated and apportioned between the flat owners (see Chapter 2).

- The recovery of expenditure under the lease: For example, to allow a landlord to be recompensed for the costs incurred in meeting their obligations under the lease.

Who can apply to a Leasehold Valuation Tribunal?

Any party to the lease, including the landlord, may make an application to a LVT. The length of the lease when originally granted must exceed 21 years, unless it was granted by a local authority or other public sector landlord as a result of a flat owner exercising their statutory right to buy; in which case, the lease can be of any length.

The law allows a flat owner to ask a LVT not only to change their own lease but also the leases of other flat owners, if a majority agree; and if it would be sensible for them all to be changed in a similar way. For example, if a LVT is being asked to require the landlord to insure the building and the other flat owners also own flats in the same block.

Applications by a large majority of leaseholders

Two or more long leases of flats can be varied by a LVT if a large majority of the flat owners agree to the change and only a small minority object.

If the application relates to eight or fewer leases, all, or all but one, of the parties, including the landlord, must agree to the application. If the application relates to more than eight leases, at least 75 per cent of the parties concerned must consent to it, and it must not be opposed by more than ten per cent of them.

The application must refer to long leases of flats held from the same landlord, but the flats do not have to be in the same building, and the leases do not have to be drafted in identical terms.

The LVT may only be willing to vary the lease in the way requested by a flat owner if compensation is paid to the landlord (for example, if the variation would cause the landlord financial loss). The LVT may also insist on the lease being changed to allow the landlord to recover the cost of any new obligations from the flat owner as part of the service charge.

It would only be sensible to make an application to the LVT if the change you want is an important one. The LVT will normally expect you to have first tried to get the lease changed by agreement with your landlord. Your first step should be to write to the landlord to find out if they will agree to the change(s) you want. Always keep copies of any letters in case you need them subsequently.

What happens when leases expire?

All leases come to an end sometime and when drafted, set out the length of the term in years and its starting date. The exact date of expiry, if not explicitly stated, can easily be determined. A flat owner with a long fixed-term lease is often described as an 'owner-occupier', and is regarded as having more in common with a freehold house owner than with a tenant. Their main worry is more likely to be whether they can meet the mortgage payments and the other costs associated with property ownership, than whether the landlord is likely to repossess their flat. If there are 90 years left to run on a lease, what is going to happen when that term ends appears a remote prospect. When there are only five years left, though, it will be a real cause for concern. If the flat owner wishes to sell, they may find it impossible to get a decent price. Or the flat owner may not be sure if they will be able to remain in their home when their lease expires.

In many cases a lease will never expire. A flat owner may negotiate a new lease with their landlord before the expiry date. Or they may exercise their statutory rights to acquire a new lease (see Chapter 5); or to purchase the freehold of their block collectively, which is often followed by the new owners granting themselves lease extensions (see Chapter 3). The extension of flat owners' rights by the 1993 Leasehold Reform, Housing and Urban Development Act has made it much less likely that long leases will ever expire. Nevertheless some will.

Prior to the mid-1950s, there was no statutory protection for long leaseholders on the termination of their lease: the situation was governed by the common law. The 1954 Landlord and Tenant Act introduced provisions giving long leaseholders similar protection to that already available to periodic and short fixed-term tenants under the Rent Acts. The Rent Acts were superseded much later by the 1988 Housing Act, which introduced the assured tenancy regime into the private sector.

Correspondingly, new provisions were introduced to govern long leases granted after the enactment of the 1988 Housing Act. These provisions are contained in the 1989 Local Government and Housing Act. This would have meant that there were two codes affecting long leases running in parallel for many years into the next century. The 1989 Act foresaw this and provided a cut-off point. From 15 January 1999, virtually all long leases are governed by the 1989 Act, regardless of when they were granted.

This means that a flat owner is able to remain in occupation when their lease comes to an end, subject to certain exceptions. Although the landlord may want the flat owner to vacate the premises, the flat owner will be able to remain in lawful occupation unless the landlord ends the long tenancy in accordance with the provisions of the 1989 Act. The landlord is only able to get a possession order from a court, necessary for lawful eviction, on one or more of the grounds specified in the Act. This is, of course, not as good as another fixed-term long lease, but it is better than being made homeless.

A landlord must serve a notice on the flat owner stating whether they propose to create an assured periodic tenancy or intend to seek possession of the flat. The flat owner has two months to respond to a landlord's notice proposing an assured tenancy. In this case, new terms would have to be settled between the former flat owner and the landlord. If you cannot agree on the terms including the rent, the landlord may apply to a Rent Assessment Committee to decide what those terms should be. Alternatively, the landlord may apply for possession of the property when the long lease ends, or at any time afterwards. Briefly, the main grounds for possession which are likely to apply when a long lease ends are:

Mandatory

- The landlord intends to demolish or reconstruct the whole or a substantial part of the building.

Discretionary

- Suitable alternative accommodation is offered to the former flat owner.

- Some rent arrears.

- Persistent delay in payment of rent.

- Breach of obligation of the tenancy.

- Deterioration of condition of the property.

- Causing nuisance or annoyance to adjoining occupiers; or being convicted of using the property for immoral or illegal purposes.

- Domestic violence.

- The accommodation is wanted for the landlord or a close relative of the landlord.

Under the discretionary grounds, a court will only evict a former flat owner if it is reasonable to do so. If the landlord fails to establish any of the grounds for possession, the former flat owner is entitled to remain in possession and go on living there. Many leases affected by this legislation will not be coming to an end for a long time. The vast majority of flat owners will have been able to exercise their rights to the collective purchase of the freehold, (see Chapter 3) or to acquire a new lease (see Chapter 5).

Ground rents and forfeiture

Ground rents

Most leases – with the exception of those specifying a 'peppercorn' – require ground rent to be paid, whether or not the landlord demands payment. Many landlords do not bother to ask for payment and then, when flat owners forget to pay, demand an additional payment. These additional payments are often excessive, and sometimes landlords also threaten further costs and legal proceedings if the additional charge and ground rent are not paid. Recognising this, the 2002 Commonhold and Leasehold Reform Act provides that:

- A flat owner is only liable for ground rent if they have received a written notice from the landlord containing certain information.
- The date the payment has to be made must be at least 30 days – and not more than 60 days – after the day the notice is given, and must not be before the date it would normally be payable under the terms of the lease.
- The landlord is prevented from making any additional charge, unless they have issued a written notice and the ground rent is still unpaid after the due date.
- The landlord is prevented from starting forfeiture action (see later) unless they have issued a written notice and the ground rent remains unpaid.

Forfeiture

Landlords usually have a right to 'forfeit' (put an end to) the lease and recover possession of their property. Most long leases contain a clause saying that the landlord is entitled to 'forfeit' the lease (ie to re-enter and take possession of the property) if the flat owner fails to comply with any of its terms. Forfeiture is not available unless there is such a clause. Forfeiture is the legal term used when a landlord attempts to bring a lease to an end before it would normally expire. It is of special importance in long leases which, unlike other kinds of tenancy, cannot be ended by a notice to quit. But it is a very severe penalty when someone's home could, in theory, be lost without compensation because of a debt of a few pounds.

Although most leases state that a landlord is entitled to 're-enter' the premises, a landlord cannot do this in practice because of the rules governing eviction. The 1977 Protection from Eviction Act requires a landlord who wishes to end a lease to first go to a court to get a possession order. It is a criminal offence, punishable by fine or imprisonment, for a landlord to evict or – attempt to evict – a flat owner without first going to court.

A flat owner who has been illegally evicted can get a court to reinstate them in their home and can also claim damages from their landlord. In some circumstances these can be substantial. There are a host of other obstacles that a landlord has to surmount before legal proceedings can be commenced. There are also a number of opportunities during the legal proceedings for the flat owner to put things right and avoid forfeiture of the lease.

Section 146 notices

In order to obtain forfeiture of a lease, a landlord has to serve a notice on the flat owner under s146 of the 1925 Law of Property Act.

In practice, forfeiture rarely happens. So before you start to panic just because you have forgotten to make your last service charge payment, it should be emphasised that forfeiture is not primarily used nowadays as a means of ending a lease and evicting a flat owner. It is a legal process allowing a landlord to enforce their rights and, in particular, to recover debts.

However, some landlords have attempted to take advantage of flat owners' fears about the costs of legal proceedings and the possibility – however distant – of losing their homes by, for example, demanding the payment of unreasonable charges; often linked to minor or non-existent breaches of the lease. Even if a landlord does go to court to forfeit the lease, because of its potentially far reaching effects, several Acts of Parliament offer protection to flat owners. These were augmented by the 2002 Commonhold and Leasehold Reform Act. They provide that:

- A landlord is only able to commence forfeiture proceedings if a court or Leasehold Valuation Tribunal (LVT) has decided that a breach of covenant or condition of the lease has occurred.

- A landlord must then serve a notice before exercising the right to forfeit a lease. This cannot be served until 14 days after a final decision has been made. It must specify the breach of the lease and give the flat owner the opportunity to remedy the breach, or to compensate the landlord for the impact of the breach.

- Forfeiture is not available as a remedy to a landlord for trivial debts that consist of ground rent, service or administration charges (or a combination of them) where the debt does not exceed £350; unless all or any part of the sum has been outstanding for more than three years.

- Forfeiture action cannot be started for non-payment of service charges unless the charge has been either agreed or admitted by the flat owner, or decided by a court, tribunal or arbitration (see Chapter 2).

- If forfeiture proceedings are brought for arrears of ground rent or service charges, the proceedings are automatically stopped if all money owing (including the landlord's legal costs) is paid into the court at least five days before the hearing.

- Even after a court hearing to forfeit a lease, a flat owner still has four weeks to pay all the money due. If the money is paid within the time limit, the lease continues as before. If the money is not paid within that time, the lease is brought to an end and a flat owner can be lawfully evicted.

- If a landlord goes to court for the breach of any other clause in the lease, a court has wide discretion to stop the lease from being brought to an end. This is usually done if the flat owner has stopped breaking the terms of the lease and promises not to do so again in the future.

Example

A flat owner agreed to pay by instalments to cover the cost of work to his block's footpaths. Because he felt the work was unsatisfactory, although the landlord disagreed, he stopped making his payments. The landlord responded by asking for the full amount owing and threatened forfeiture if it was not paid. The flat owner offered to recommence his instalments but the landlord refused to accept them and again threatened forfeiture.

Forfeiture is extremely rare if the breach can be, or is, remedied. But landlords sometimes try to exploit the threat of forfeiture. If your landlord is threatening you with forfeiture proceedings, you should seek expert advice from a solicitor or other adviser quickly. There may be a defence that you are unaware of. But if you defend a case and lose, you may have to pay your landlord's legal costs as well as your own, and may even lose your home too.

It is usually sensible to avoid or delay the prospect of your landlord starting forfeiture procedures. If there are sums that you accept that you owe, you should pay. This will reduce the risk of you becoming liable for your landlords' legal costs, which could be considerable, and possibly more than the amount you owe. In certain circumstances, a flat owner can legally withhold payment of a service charge (see Chapter 2).

Mortgage arrears

Mortgages are loans secured against property. This means a flat owner can lose their home if they do not make regular repayments to their mortgage lender. Lenders can take action to evict a flat owner who is in arrears with their repayments. There is less protection for a flat owner in mortgage arrears than there is in connection with forfeiture. But a flat owner cannot be evicted for arrears without a court order. Before legal proceedings can start, the lender will normally make a written demand for any arrears, followed by a formal demand for repayment of the whole of the outstanding debt. The next step is for the lender to start a possession case in court (usually a county court, but some mortgage cases are started in the High Court). A court does not have to grant a possession order immediately. It can grant a suspended order on condition that the flat owner restarts repayments and there are arrangements to clear the arrears (possibly over many years).

If you are having trouble making your regular mortgage repayments, take action without delay. Contact your mortgage lender. Lenders are expected to treat arrears sympathetically. Mortgages can be rearranged to reduce or defer repayments. If you are in financial hardship, seek help. You may be able to claim on insurance, or claim income support, to cover part of what you owe. Most advice centres offer help to people with serious debt problems.

Service charges

2

Introduction

Long residential leases usually require flat owners to make two different kinds of regular payment to their landlord:

* ground rent; and
* a service charge.

A flat owner may also be asked to pay administration charges. These are explained on page 141.

Ground rents are perhaps the most recognisable feature of a long residential lease (see Chapter 1). A ground rent is a relatively small payment that your lease requires you to pay to your landlord every year. Service charges are sometimes known as 'maintenance charges', 'service rent' or 'additional rent', but by law they are different from rent.

Flat owners are responsible for the internal repair, upkeep and decoration of their own flat. Usually their landlord is responsible under the terms of the lease for repairs and maintenance to the building or block and to any common parts, such as a hall, a lift or garden, and to keep the property insured. The lease may require or permit the landlord to provide other services, such as a caretaker. The lease may also permit the landlord to make improvements to the building or estate.

The landlord is allowed to recover the costs of all of these repairs and services as service charges. The usual arrangement is that each of the flat owners pays a contribution to the costs, and these contributions add up to 100 per cent of the costs.

The contributions may add up to less than 100 per cent if the landlord uses part of the block or estate or lets out flats on short residential tenancies (for example, a council estate).

The service charge is often the largest item of regular expenditure a flat owner has to meet, other than their mortgage payment. Service charges are often administered and collected by a managing agent who acts on the landlord's behalf. A managing agent will also include their administrative costs in the service charge. Where there is no managing agent, the lease may allow the landlord to charge for administrative costs.

Leases usually require a service charge to be paid annually, or, more often, quarterly or monthly. Unlike a ground rent, a service charge is generally variable from year to year according to the particular services provided. It is common to pay either a standard amount fixed by the lease, or an amount to cover the estimated costs for the coming year. Then at the end of the year, when the actual costs are known, the account is balanced. If the flat owner has paid too much, the balance is usually credited against the bill for the next year, and if too little, then the flat owner is billed.

Flat owners often complain that their service charge is excessive, or that they are not getting value for money. Some also report that it is difficult to find out what their service charge contributions are actually being spent on. There are several stages in finding out how much a landlord may charge for services.

First, it is necessary to check the lease itself, which should state what items are covered and how the charge is calculated. Second, flat owners are entitled by law to obtain information about their service charge. Third, the law imposes limits on what can be charged, and the procedures to be followed. And, fourth, flat owners can challenge a service charge on a number of grounds.

This chapter explains a flat owner's rights in relation to service charges, including:

- Service charges and leases.
- Information about service charges.

- The amount of the service charge.
- Reserve funds.
- Demands for payment.
- Challenging service charges.

Service charges and leases

The basic rule is that the cost of an item cannot be recovered from a flat owner unless the lease permits it. If you pay service charges, your lease will set out the items of expenditure for which you are liable. Your lease will also state what share of the overall charge for the block you will be required to pay. Any advance payment must be of a reasonable amount. Your lease may also allow your landlord to operate a 'reserve' or 'sinking fund' towards future large items of expenditure (see Reserve funds, page 68).

You will generally have to pay for services even if you do not take advantage of them. For example, you may live on the ground floor, but have to pay for the maintenance of a lift.

The general rule is that a landlord can only charge for something that he or she can show is allowed by the lease. If a lease is not explicit on a particular point, it may be that a particular charge could be implied, but only where the wording allows it. If the lease was poorly written, the service charge may not include, for example, the cost of major works, or the cost of structural repairs outside the common parts.

Some leases have very broad clauses allowing a landlord to provide any services they think fit. This may allow the landlord to, for example, introduce and charge for a caretaker against a flat owner's wishes. However, the costs of such a service must be reasonable, and the standard of the service must also be reasonable (see Amount of service charge, page 62). Ideally, your solicitor should have drawn your attention to such a wide clause at the time of purchase.

The landlord can only recover interest on a loan raised to carry out repairs if the lease provides for this.

The landlord may make a management charge as part of the service charge. Where this is simply the fee of a surveyor or other managing agent, it is relatively straightforward. Where the landlord wants to recover their own management costs, only the real cost is chargeable, and this is not intended to allow the landlord to make a profit. Management costs are subject to challenge in the same way as the rest of the service charge.

A typical lease will usually require some or all of the service charge to be paid in advance and will fix a reckoning point – often at the end of the financial or calendar year – when the precise amount is calculated and the balance credited or invoiced to the flat owner. Sometimes, the lease allows any surplus to remain in a reserve fund. If the lease does not require some of the service charge to be paid in advance, a landlord is only entitled to be paid after the service or work has been provided or done, or the money has been spent (see Amount of service charge, page 62 for the limitations imposed by statute). Money may be payable in advance, subject to the trust fund arrangements made mandatory in April 1989 (see Reserve funds, page 68).

It should be noted that a clause allowing the landlord to set aside funds is just that: a power to put aside some of the service charge income in the year in which it was collected. It is not a power to levy charges in advance for major works. A specific clause on reserve funds is necessary for this, which is subject to the trust fund arrangements (see Reserve funds, page 68).

Your lease should also specify how the service charge is calculated and apportioned between individual flat owners. The simplest system takes the total costs incurred in the relevant year and then divides this sum by the number of flats in the building. However, some leases use other systems; for example, dividing the costs according to the floor area of the flats. In some buildings, some flats may have more restricted services, for example, more restricted access to the common parts than others and so may pay less for services to them.

Another common method of calculating a service charge is to make it proportionate to the old rateable value of the individual flats or, increasingly, to a flat's council tax band. On large estates, some costs may be divided across the whole estate, while other costs are divided only among the flats in one particular building. Whichever system is used, it should be set out in your lease, and your landlord should use that system.

Where the lease fails to make satisfactory provision for repairs, maintenance or service charges, a flat owner or landlord may ask the Leasehold Valuation Tribunal (see page 164) to change the provisions in the lease. Typical examples of leases that may be varied are where the lease is unclear as to who has the duty to repair, or where the service charge proportions do not add up to 100 per cent. Such variations often require the majority of those concerned to agree to the application (See Varying leases, page 41).

Information about service charges

Flat owners can require their landlord to provide them with information about service charges using statutory rights (1985 Landlord and Tenant Act, as amended by the 1987 Landlord and Tenant Act and the 1996 Housing Act). You can write to your landlord, either directly or care of the landlord's agent, requesting a written summary of costs incurred in the last service charge accounting year. The secretary of a recognised tenants' association (see Tenants' associations, page 121) can make the request on behalf of all the flat owners. If the accounts are not made up on an annual basis, which is unlikely, then you or the secretary can request a written summary for the year ending at the date of the request.

Your landlord must supply the summary either within one month of the request, or within six months of the end of the relevant year, whichever is the later. The summary has to show how the costs incurred have been, or will be, reflected in service charges. It must show which costs, if any, are ones for which the landlord has not had a bill in the relevant year; which costs have been billed but not yet paid; and which were billed and paid. It must also show the total amount received from the flat owners in advance payment of service charge that is still standing to their credit at the end of the relevant year.

If the owners of more than four flats in a block are contributing to the same costs in service charges, then a qualified accountant has to certify that the written summary is fair and supported by accounts, receipts and other documents. The accountant may not be an officer, managing agent, employee or partner of your landlord.

A landlord who fails without good reason to provide a summary or supporting documents when requested, is guilty of a criminal offence. Local authorities have the power to prosecute in such cases. Summary accounts can be presented in different ways but the example on the following two pages from a small block of six flats each paying an equal service charge of £332 in 2000, shows a typical approach.

Example:

Dickens Way Management Co Ltd
Service Charge Account
For the year ended 31 March 2000

	2000	1999
Building Insurance	364	367
Electricity Charges	73	90
Communal Cleaning	51	45
Maintenance	40	79
Repairs	756	-
Decoration	-	917
Managing Agent's Fees	465	465
Audit/Accountancy Fees	385	376
Bank charges/Interest	57	45
Sundry Expenses	22	22
Fixed Assets Written Off	1	-
	2,214	2,406
Total Income	1,992	1,992
Withdrawn from Reserves	222	414

Notes to the Account

For the year ended 31 March 2000
Reconciliation of Cash Movements to Total Expenditure

Cash paid during year		1,620
Less: amounts included in previous accounting period (accruals brought forward)		(340)
Add: amounts paid in previous accounting period but not included in previous account (prepayments brought forward)		70
		1,350
Less: paid during period but not included in the account (prepayments carried forward)		(100)
Add accruals: Repairs	756	
Electricity	21	
Audit/Accountancy Fee	92	
Managing Agent's Fee	70	
Maintenance	25	964
Total Expenditure for the year		**2,214**

Within six months of getting the summary, you, or the secretary of any recognised tenants' association, may write to your landlord – either directly, or care of the landlord's agent – requiring them to provide 'reasonable facilities' to inspect and to take copies of the accounts, receipts and other documents supporting the summary. Your landlord must make the facilities available for a period of two months, starting not later than one month from the date of the request. You or the secretary are entitled to inspect the documents free of charge, and to take copies of them for a reasonable charge. Your landlord is permitted to take the costs of the inspection into account when calculating their management charge. Again, a landlord who fails to allow an inspection is guilty of a criminal offence.

There are similar provisions covering information held by a superior landlord. In particular, if part of the information is needed from a superior landlord, then the intermediate landlord is under a duty to go through a similar procedure to obtain it, and the superior landlord is under a similar duty to provide it. A failure of the intermediate landlord, or the superior landlord, to comply with their duties without good reason is a criminal offence.

Flat owners' rights have been improved by the 2002 Commonhold and Leasehold Reform Act, but these have not been implemented, and may not be, because of opposition from social landlords concerned about the costs involved. If the new rules are implemented, your landlord will have to provide an annual statement of account – whether requested or not – certified by an accountant and in a form to be set out in regulations. If you request to inspect or copy documents, these must be provided within 21 days. Your landlord will have to give you a notice of your rights and obligations about service charges when a demand for payment is sent.

Checking the information

Where the accounts are simple, or for relatively small sums, you can probably do the checking yourself. If the accounts are large and complicated, you may need professional help.

Since 1997, a recognised tenants' association can appoint a qualified surveyor to advise it on matters relating to service charges. The surveyor has the right to inspect the premises and inspect and copy documents held by the landlord. If your landlord refuses to give your surveyor access to the necessary documents, or prevents inspection of the property, the surveyor can apply to a court to force your landlord to comply. In a serious case, you would be well advised to use this right.

The 1993 Leasehold Reform, Housing and Urban Development Act introduced another way for flat owners to obtain service charge information. Provided enough flat owners – usually not less than two thirds – are prepared to support the application, a landlord can be compelled to agree to a management audit. It is necessary to appoint a qualified accountant or surveyor to carry out such an audit.

The purpose of the audit is to find out if the landlord's management obligations are being performed in an efficient and effective manner, and if the service charges are being spent properly. The auditor has statutory rights to inspect the necessary documents. A court can compel a landlord to comply with a management audit. This right is very powerful but less easy to use than the rights to obtain information.

If it is subsequently decided to challenge some aspect of a landlord's management practices, evidence from an audit will be taken into account and compared with the applicable standard of good management practice, set out in the relevant Government approved code (see Chapter 6).

Amount of service charge

The 1985 Landlord and Tenant Act contains limitations on the amount that a flat owner must pay as a service charge. Generally, this statute overrides a lease if there is a conflict. The law defines 'service charges' to mean an amount payable by a tenant (flat owner) of a dwelling as part of, or in addition to, rent

- which is payable, directly or indirectly, for services, repairs, maintenance, insurance or the landlord's costs of management, and, since 30 September 2003, for improvements; and
- the whole or part of which varies, or may vary, according to the relevant costs.

Amounts are only payable if the lease states that they are. Relevant costs include estimated costs and have to be in connection with the matters for which the service charge is payable, including overheads. Costs are still relevant, even if they are for a period other than the current service charge year but see Demands for payment, page 70.

The law provides some control over the level of charge. 'Relevant costs' can only be taken into account in working out the service charge to the extent that they are 'reasonably incurred', and only where they are for services or works of a 'reasonable standard'. Payments in advance also have to be reasonable. There has to be a reckoning after the costs have been incurred, and any balance either refunded to the flat owner or used to reduce charges in subsequent years. The legislation also declares that a clause in a lease that states that 'the landlord can decide what is reasonable' is void. You may agree that a particular sum is reasonable, but simply by paying a service charge demand, you are not admitting that it is all reasonable. If you and your landlord cannot agree what is reasonable, you can ask the Leasehold Valuation Tribunal to decide (see page 164).

Example

Five flat owners have flats in a large house. The landlord's annual bill for service charges includes £600 per flat for cleaning the hall and stairs – a total of £3,000 for the house. The flat owners know the cleaner only visits for an hour once a week and because the vacuum cleaner has been broken for the past year and the landlord has not had it repaired, the cleaner has not actually cleaned the carpets. The flat owners have vacuumed the hall and stairs themselves. In that year, therefore, the charge of £3,000 is not a reasonable relevant cost and the cleaning services are not of a reasonable standard. The flat owners are not legally bound to each pay £600; even though cleaning charges are specified in the lease and the landlord's agents have included the sum in the bill; and claim that it is reasonable.

Consultation

The landlord must consult you and other flat owners before committing to large expenses. If the landlord fails to consult, then you may not be liable for the charges on which you should have been consulted. Note that consultation means giving you information and an opportunity to express your opinion; but it does not necessarily mean accepting your opinion or even the opinion of most – or all – of the flat owners.

Some leases contain a duty for the landlord to consult. If the landlord fails to consult about a specific item, you may not have to pay for that item.

Landlords must consult where required to do so by statute. There were requirements under the 1985 Landlord and Tenant Act, but these were replaced by requirements in the 2002 Commonhold and Leasehold Reform Act. This happened on 31 October 2003 in England, and on 30 March 2004 in Wales. The old rules applied to consultations before these dates.

Consultation before 2003/4

If the costs were before the above dates, the landlord should have consulted about 'major works' costing more than the 'prescribed amount' of £50 per dwelling; or more than £1,000 in total. The required procedure to be followed depended on whether there was a recognised association representing the flat owners or not (see Tenants' associations, page 121).

If there was a recognised tenants' association
1. The landlord gave the association's secretary a notice with a detailed specification of the proposed works, allowing a reasonable period for the association to suggest the names of contractors who might be asked to provide estimates. The landlord did not need to accept any suggestions made by the association.

2. At least two estimates were obtained and at least one of the estimates was from a contractor wholly unconnected with the landlord. A copy of each was given to the association's secretary.

3. Each flat owner was sent a notice briefly describing the proposed works; summarising the estimates (or enclosing copies of the estimates themselves); and informing them that they can inspect and take copies of the detailed job specification and estimates. The notice asked for comments to be sent to a specified address within a period of not less than one month. Unless the works are urgent, they could not begin until the time given by the landlord for comments had run out. The landlord had to take into consideration any comments made by the flat owners.

If there was no recognised tenants' association

1. At least two estimates were obtained for the work and at least one was from a contractor wholly unconnected with the landlord.

2. Each flat owner was sent a notice describing the proposed works, accompanied by copies of the estimates. The notice asked for comments to be sent to a specified address within a period of not less than one month. As an alternative to sending each flat owner an individual notice, a notice and copy estimates could be displayed where all the flat owners were likely to see them.

3. The landlord must 'have regard' to any comments received. Unless the works are urgent, they cannot begin until the time given by the landlord for comments has run out.

The sanction for not complying with the preliminary procedure is severe. Any excess in the cost, above the prescribed amount, cannot be taken into account when calculating the service charge. A court or Leasehold Valuation Tribunal has discretion to dispense with all or any of the requirements, if it is satisfied that the landlord acted reasonably. An example might be if repairs were needed to specialised equipment, such as a lift, and only the original manufacturer maintained its products, so that obtaining a competitive estimate is impossible, or where the works were urgent.

Example

The exterior of a block of flats needs redecorating. Without warning, the landlord sends in a subsidiary company to do the work, which is delayed. The landlord did not seek estimates or give notice. The work is not urgent, as shown by the delay, and the fact that it only involves redecoration. The contractor is not independent of the landlord. The flat owners are liable to pay only the greater of £1,000 or £50 per flat. If the work is of a poor standard, then the relevant costs may not be reasonable and might be reduced even below the greater of £1,000 or £50 per flat, if it is reasonable to do so.

Consultation now

For costs incurred since the relevant dates (31 October 2003 in England and 30 March 2004 in Wales), the landlord must consult flat owners before carrying out qualifying works above a certain value, or entering into a long term agreement.

Qualifying works are proposed works of repair, maintenance or improvement that would cost any flat owner more than £250.

A long term agreement means an agreement for works or services, which will last for a period of more than 12 months; and where the cost for any flat owner exceeds £100 per year. Employment contracts are excluded.

The consultation procedure is as follows:
1. The landlord must send an initial notice to every flat owner and any recognised tenants' association that provides:
    - a general description of the work or agreement; or a place and times for inspection of the description or agreement
    - reasons for the works or agreement
    - that flat owners can make written observations within 30 days

- that flat owners and any recognised tenants' association can suggest an alternative contractor.

2. The landlord must consider any observations received, and then obtain estimates. For qualifying works, there must be at least two estimates, including at least one from a contractor unconnected with the landlord; and at least one from a contractor proposed by a flat owner or association. For a long term agreement, the landlord must get estimates from the landlord's proposed contractor and any alternative contractor proposed by a flat owner or association.

3. The landlord must give further notice to the flat owners and the association, stating:

   - the estimates
   - identity of proposed contractor
   - any connection between landlord and proposed contractor
   - if a long term agreement with a managing agent is proposed, whether the agent is a member of a professional body
   - if a long term agreement is proposed, how long it is expected to last, and the likely cost per flat (or total expenditure if cost per flat cannot be calculated)
   - a summary of flat owners' observations and the landlord's response
   - that flat owners can make written observations within 30 days.

4. If the landlord accepts one of the estimates for qualifying works, or makes the long term agreement, the landlord must inform flat owners and any association within 21 days, giving reasons, or stating where and when such reasons may be inspected. The landlord should also summarise any further observations received and respond to them. This last notice is unnecessary when the contractor was nominated by a flat owner or association; or had submitted the lowest estimate.

If the landlord fails to follow the consultation procedure, he or she can only recover up to £250 per flat owner for qualifying works, and up to £100 per flat owner for a long term agreement. The Leasehold Valuation Tribunal can allow the landlord to proceed without consultation in an urgent case, and still recover all the costs.

Where there is a long term agreement in place, and the landlord wants to carry out works that will cost more than £250 for any flat owner under that agreement, there is a limited further requirement for consultation. The landlord must send a notice to tenants and any recognised tenants' association that provides:

- a general description of the works in general terms, or a place and times for inspection of the description
- reasons for the works
- an estimate of total expenditure on the works
- that flat owners and any recognised tenants' association can make written observations within 30 days.

There is no right to nominate an alternative contractor and, following receipt of observations, the landlord's requirement is to respond within 21 days to the maker of the observations.

If your landlord is a council or other public authority, then very large contracts and works are subject to European Union rules, and the consultation procedure may be different.

Reserve funds

The arrangements for funding the maintenance and repair of a block of flats may include building up a reserve or 'sinking' fund from contributions included in the annual service charge. The purpose is to ensure that money is available for major items of expenditure, without excessive fluctuations in the service charge from one year to the next. Items that could be a call on such a fund are exterior redecoration, or the replacement of boilers and lifts.

Under the 1987 Landlord and Tenant Act, a reserve fund must be held on 'trust' for the contributing flat owners. This applies to all service charges, but is most important in relation to reserve funds. If two or more flat owners are paying towards the same costs in service charges, then the sums paid must be held by the person who received them (for example, a landlord) in one or more trust funds, unless the landlord is a local authority or other social housing organisation, such as a housing association. If a flat owner's lease sets up a different arrangement, the 1987 Act overrides the lease, unless the lease specifically set up a trust covering the funds before April 1989.

Trust funds have to be invested in a limited range of secure investments, and any interest or other income accrued has to be paid into the trust account. The funds have to be held on trust for the flat owners as the beneficiaries, to meet the cost of the works or services for which they are paid. If there is any money left over after the costs for which the funds are earmarked have been incurred, the balance belongs to the flat owners in proportion to the sums they contributed towards the service charges.

If a flat owner sells their property and moves, they are not usually entitled to a share of the balance of the trust fund. A flat owner's contributions remain on trust for future leaseholders. Moreover, if at the time a lease ends there are no more flat owners contributing to the same costs, then the landlord gets the assets of the trust fund(s), unless the lease provides otherwise.

The main advantage of the trust fund arrangements is that if a landlord or a managing agent becomes insolvent, the funds cannot be used to pay their debts. If a landlord or an agent misappropriates the funds, the flat owners can take them to court for breach of trust.

Flat owners are entitled to be given accounts showing where the money has been invested, how much is being made from the investments and proof that the income has been ploughed back into the fund. Flat owners should also be entitled to see any documents supporting these accounts. In any event, leases should provide for this information to be given.

A landlord who sells their interest in the property to another landlord is apparently under no obligation to transfer the trust funds to the new landlord. Leases should, but may not, put a specific obligation on the old landlord to allow the new landlord to take over the funds. The law is also vague about what should happen to the trust funds if they cannot be used for works or services but the leases continue; for example, the building has burnt down and cannot be rebuilt. In this situation, leases should, but again may not, provide for the funds to be distributed between the flat owners, in proportion to the amounts they paid in.

In many blocks there is a fairly rapid turnover of residents as existing owners sell and new owners move in. The problem thus arises of how to share out more equitably the cost of expensive works over time. Reserve funds, properly managed, are a sensible and practical method of spreading the cost out more fairly between former and current flat owners.

Provisions in the 2002 Commonhold and Leasehold Reform Act that are not yet in force require credit balances to be put in specified accounts; allow flat owners to inspect documents to check it has been done; and introduce a criminal offence for failure to comply.

Demands for payment

A written service charge demand must contain certain basic information if the amount demanded is to be lawfully payable (1987 Landlord and Tenant Act). It must state the name and address of the landlord. If that address is not in England or Wales, an address that is must be given for service on the landlord (see Information about your landlord, page 118).

There is a time limit for making service charge demands. Flat owners are not normally liable to pay any charge relating to costs incurred more than 18 months before they received the demand. They do have to pay, if during that period their landlord sent them a notice saying that costs had been incurred and that a demand would be sent later.

Challenging service charges

If you are considering challenging the amount of – or a specific item in – a service charge, remember that the landlord needs to carry out repairs and maintenance for the benefit of flat owners, and usually needs to recover the costs of doing so. If flat owners make the procedure or recovery of costs unnecessarily difficult, necessary work may be delayed or avoided, and the eventual cost may be much higher.

While undoubtedly some landlords overcharge, and some carry out unnecessary work, there are also many landlords who do too little work, and as a result, their buildings are decaying. The end result can be large repair bills in the future and/or a reduction in the value of your flat.

When you first get involved in a dispute, and at every stage during the dispute, you should consider the factors listed in Chapter 8 (page 162). Remember that it is usually best if all the flat owners act together, preferably through a recognised tenants' association (see Tenants' associations, page 121).

It is important to keep copies of all correspondence sent and received. If the basis of the complaint relates to the provision or the standard of a service or services, flat owners should keep a diary or record of services provided and not provided. All complaints should be made in writing, dated, and copies kept, in order to show that the landlord or the agent was made aware of any failure in the provision or the standard of the service. The courts have decided that a landlord who contracts to provide a service should do so, even if the flat owner is in arrears.

Example

Suppose a group of flat owners have decided to claim that the charges for central heating are unreasonable because the system does not work properly. In such a case, it would be advisable to keep a daily record of the dates, and perhaps the internal air temperatures, during the relevant

period, say October to March. All the flat owners, or at any
rate a majority of them, should keep a record.

The usual first stage is to raise the problem with your landlord
or managing agent. You may need more information, and can
either ask for this, or formally exercise the right to obtain information
explained on page 57 above. If the records seem unreliable, you may
wish to request a management audit (see page 61). If your landlord
fails to comply, then you might ask your local authority to prosecute.

The second stage should be to try to negotiate a more
reasonable figure with your landlord or agent, if it is apparent
from the information supplied or discovered that the demand
is unreasonable. At this stage it might be worth consulting an
independent professional, perhaps to get a report prepared or an
alternative estimate, although you should weigh the cost of such
professional services against the amount under dispute.

If you are unable to reach full agreement with your landlord, the
third stage is to decide whether to proceed further, bearing in
mind the amount still under dispute and, if so, which route to take.
There are a number of possible options:

1. The Leasehold Valuation Tribunal (LVT) will handle most
   service charge disputes that cannot be resolved between the
   parties. You should consider the options at number 3 first.

2. Legal action in a county court. Nowadays, it will not usually
   be appropriate to take a service charge dispute to court.
   Sometimes a landlord will start a court action if service
   charge is not being paid, and if there is a genuine dispute, the
   court will usually transfer that dispute to the LVT.

3. Use some other dispute resolution procedure, for example:
   - arbitration
   - complaints procedure
   - mediation
   - resolution by a third party
   - keep negotiating.

Your lease may state a particular method of resolving disputes. Some of these are binding. For example, if your lease says that an arbitrator must determine service charge disputes if not agreed, that will probably prevent an application to the LVT or court. It will not prevent negotiation or mediation taking place. However, if your lease says that the landlord or the managing agent has the final say about service charges, this is not correct. Service charges can always be reviewed by the LVT, court or (if the lease requires) arbitrator.

See Chapter 8 for further information about resolving disputes.

Buying your building under the 1993 Act

3

Introduction

It has always been possible for flat owners, either individually or collectively, to purchase the freehold of the building or block they live in, provided their landlord wishes to sell. Around 40 per cent of all flat owners in England already own all, or part of their building freehold. Many landlords do not relish the duties expected of them; especially in return for what some regard as a meagre income. Many commercial developers of blocks of flats have no desire to retain an interest in, or manage, a property once the flats have been sold. Very often such developers solve this problem by granting very long leases and vesting the freehold reversion to those leases in a flat management company (see Chapter 7). Sometimes people inherit the freehold of a residential block. Either way they have no wish to hang on to it.

Many owners of blocks of flats do not want to sell their freeholds. Some derive a considerable income from their leasehold properties. In 1967, Parliament gave the leaseholders of houses the right to buy their freehold. With regard to flats, the breakthrough finally occurred in 1987. This right was extended in 1993 when flat owners were given a right to buy the freehold of their block as a group – a process known as 'collective enfranchisement' – whether their landlord agreed or not. Under this legislation – the 1993 Leasehold Reform, Housing and Urban Development Act – flat owners were also given a right to have their lease extended (see Chapter 5). Some defects in the 1993 Act were subsequently rectified by the 1996 Housing Act, and in the 2002 Commonhold and Leasehold Reform Act.

The purpose of this most important change in English and Welsh housing law was to meet the two main perceived problems with long leases of flats. First, a lease is a 'wasting asset' and over time it becomes increasingly difficult to mortgage a leasehold flat; thus affecting the property market and population mobility. Second, not all landlords are good landlords. Some are difficult to contact; others fail to carry out their repairing and other obligations; and some attempt to overcharge for services. If flat owners can buy the freehold of their block, they can grant themselves new leases, solving the first problem; and run their own management services, solving the second.

The 1987 Landlord and Tenant Act had earlier given flat owners a more limited 'right of first refusal'. It requires a landlord who intends to sell their interest in a block of flats to first offer it to the block's residents (see Chapter 4). In addition, flat residents have a right to buy their landlord's interest compulsorily at any time, if a property has been seriously mismanaged (see Chapter 6). Although in many respects the rights under the 1987 Act have been replaced by those of the 1993 Act, it remains on the statute book and, in some circumstances, purchase under it is possible when it is not available under the 1993 legislation. A purchase under the 1987 Act can also often be cheaper than one under the 1993 Act.

This chapter looks at:

- The benefits of buying your freehold.
- Purchase under the 'collective enfranchisement' provisions of the 1993 Leasehold Reform, Housing and Urban Development Act.
- Getting organised for purchase.
- The likely costs of buying the freehold.

The benefits of buying your freehold

Why should flat owners go to the trouble and expense of buying their freehold? After all they will still have a lease to their flat after the process is completed. Nevertheless, there are a number of identifiable advantages, and some disadvantages, which owners should consider before coming to a decision. These include:

- After purchase, you will have the power to grant longer leases without having to pay.

- If there are problems with your existing leases, you may be able collectively to vary the terms of the leases. There would be no need to go to court or tribunal to do this.

- You can together decide what is a reasonable service charge and you will be in a better position to ensure that you get value for money.

- You can together choose to carry out improvements to the building, or add new amenities such as parking areas or recreational facilities.

- You will be able to decide collectively whether or not to appoint managing agents and to replace them if you are unhappy with their performance.

- You may find that your flat increases in value.

- You may find that it is easier to sell your flat if you own a share in the freehold.

These potential benefits need to be balanced against a number of drawbacks:

- Purchase may prove to be costly, awkward and lengthy.

- Unless you employ managing agents, you may find that being a member of the purchaser company is a time-consuming business.

- If you become a director of the new company, you may sometimes have to make decisions that prove unpopular with your neighbours. For further information on flat management companies, see Chapter 7.

- You might have to face directly some of the problems of leasehold property management – dealing with service charge arrears, nuisance residents, 'cowboy' builders etc.

The impact of leasehold reform

In 1996, an early assessment of leasehold reform was made on behalf of the Government. While only four per cent of leaseholders in the sample had progressed to enfranchisement using the formal procedures, 16 per cent had bought their freeholds informally. Another 14 per cent were still attempting to enfranchise. Most of the remainder were either still undecided whether to proceed, or had suspended their interest in enfranchisement altogether. Another five per cent had completed the lease extension process (see Chapter 5).

Which tenants qualify?

The right to enfranchise (and to extend a lease; see Chapter 5) is given to those flat owners known as 'qualifying tenants'. This means a flat owner must have a long lease. A long lease is one that was originally granted for more than 21 years. A shorter lease may qualify as 'long' if it is renewable by the leaseholder. There was previously an additional low rent test, but this was abolished by the 1996 Housing Act and the 2002 Commonhold and Leasehold Reform Act.

There are some exceptions. A flat owner cannot be a qualifying tenant if:

- the landlord is a charitable housing trust (this includes many housing associations) and the flat is provided as part of its charitable work; or
- the lease is a business lease, even where it includes residential parts of the premises.

Generally speaking, you do not have to live in your flat to be a qualifying tenant. There are however, two special rules that mean that some non-residents are not qualifying tenants, despite owning flats on long leases:

- Flats subject to more than one long lease: There can be only one qualifying tenant per flat. This is not a problem for joint tenants who qualify jointly. It applies where a flat has an intermediate landlord who is also a long leaseholder. In that case, the intermediate landlord is not a qualifying tenant, but the other leaseholder is the qualifying tenant.

- Persons owning several flats: Although a qualifying tenant does not have to be resident, for the purposes of enfranchisement no one can be a qualifying tenant of more than two flats in the same building. If someone owns more than two flats, they are not a qualifying tenant of any of them. They may still be a qualifying tenant for lease renewal (see Chapter 5) but not for enfranchisement.

Which properties?

A single flat is part of a larger building or block. Under the 1993 Act, it is the block that is enfranchised – there is no right to buy the freehold of an individual flat. Flat owners have to join together to force the sale of their freehold.

A building can be enfranchised if it contains at least two flats and is either detached, or vertically divided, from neighbouring buildings and structurally self-contained. No part of it must be built on top of, or beneath any other property, and it must be capable of being redeveloped on its own.

If there is more than one freeholder of your building, this will not usually prevent enfranchisement from taking place, but it is important to establish who all of the freeholders are (see Discovery notice at page 81).

There are three tests of eligibility for buildings:

- Mainly long leasehold: At least two-thirds of the flats must be owned by qualifying tenants. In a building where two-thirds of the number of flats is not a whole number, the fraction involved has to be rounded up to find the qualifying threshold.

- Mainly residential: No more than 25 per cent of the floor space (apart from common parts such as stairs) can be in non-residential use. Non-residential use includes shops, offices, workshops and also garages/storage units, unless they are intended for the use of flat owners. So a block of flats with shops taking up all of its ground floor will probably have to be at least four storeys high to qualify.

- Small converted buildings with a resident freeholder: If a property was converted at some time (not a purpose built block of flats) contains four or fewer flats, is in the same ownership as when converted; and the freeholder or an adult member of his immediate family has lived in one of the flats as their only or main home for the last 12 months; it is not eligible for enfranchisement. This rule does not apply if the resident landlord is a leaseholder rather than the freeholder.

'Flat' includes a maisonette and properties which do not satisfy certain rules of the 1967 Leasehold Reform Act which gave the leaseholders of houses the right to buy their freehold.

Property exemptions under the 1993 Act are rare. The main exemptions are:

- Crown property is exempt, although generally the Crown authorities permit enfranchisement and lease extensions (see Chapter 5), as if the 1993 Act applied to it.

- Certain heritage properties, such as properties owned by the National Trust, are exempt from both enfranchisement and lease extensions (see Chapter 5).

- Some private properties that have special tax status because they are open to the public are exempt from enfranchisement; but not lease extensions (see Chapter 5).

- Properties including railway track or associated structures are exempt.

- Properties in cathedral closes are exempt from both enfranchisement and lease extensions (see Chapter 5).

The 50 per cent test

Once it is established that a building is eligible for enfranchisement, the 50 per cent of flats test must be satisfied. The tenants applying for enfranchisement must include the occupiers of half or more of all the flats in the building. Where there are only two flats, the owners of both must apply.

The additional tests of two-thirds of qualifying tenants and residency were abolished by the 2002 Commonhold and Leasehold Reform Act.

Example

Take a block of 65 flats. Twenty are occupied by non-qualifying tenants; they are secure tenants of the local authority. Thirty one (69 per cent) of the qualifying tenants support enfranchisement. But this is less than half of the occupiers of all the flats. The 50 per cent of flats test is not satisfied.

As before, fractions of whole numbers are rounded up. And as before, this can have important implications for eligibility in small blocks.

Special rules operate in the case of blocks in which two-thirds or more of the long leases are due to expire within five years. The freeholder may be able to prevent enfranchisement if there are plans to redevelop the block. Flat owners whose leases are approaching this threshold need to act quickly to preserve their right to enfranchisement.

The process

If you and your neighbours wish to buy the freehold, it is important that you obtain as much information as possible about the different types of leases, service charges, their lengths, and the owners of the individual flats in your block. The following is an outline of the different stages involved and does not cover every detail of the enfranchisement process.

Discovery notice

It may not be possible to get all the information you need other than from your landlord. In that case, the 2002 Act allows flat owners considering enfranchisement to serve a 'discovery' notice on the landlord or the managing agent, requiring them to provide:

- the name and address of the freeholder and all those who hold other interests in the building, including details of all the other leaseholders in the block; and
- details of those interests and any other relevant information.

The discovery notice does not commit you to buying the freehold. The landlord must supply the information requested within 28 days. A flat owner can serve a discovery notice on their own, so, at this stage, there is no need to get one's neighbours to agree to buy the freehold.

Tenants' response

Because enfranchisement is a group action, the other tenant(s) should be contacted at an early stage in order to decide whether to proceed or not. The rules for eligibility are complex and the first action should be to check that your building satisfies the rules, and that there are sufficient qualifying tenants to be able to continue. You should make sure that:

- Your building passes the 25 per cent commercial rule.
- You and your neighbours own at least half of the total number of flats in the building.

Example

There are 50 flats in a block. In order to enfranchise:

- The participants in an enfranchisement application must represent at least half of the flats in the block – in this case 25 flat owners is the minimum number who must participate.

Before the process can proceed, there should be, if possible, a commitment from all those who have agreed to take part, as otherwise qualifying tenants could drop out at the last minute. This commitment should, if possible, be legally binding on the participants: this is critical if the cost of enfranchisement is relatively high. This is much more important in smaller blocks than bigger ones, because the financial implications of two tenants withdrawing from a group of ten are greater than two withdrawing from a group of 50. This is because their share of the costs will have to be spread out among fewer people.

You must prepare thoroughly before committing yourselves. At some point in the action, the qualifying tenants will need to appoint a valuer and a solicitor. An initial valuation of the building is strongly advised so that you have an idea of the final purchase price before commencing the action. Once it is decided to buy the landlord's interest, you will need to agree who is to buy the property on the qualifying tenants' behalf. This person is known as your nominee purchaser. You need to decide early on how you want your building to be owned and run in the future. Your decision will help you to choose a nominee purchaser.

A nominee purchaser can be one of the flat owners or up to four as joint owners, a corporate body, a trust, or a company. In most circumstances, especially in larger blocks, a flat management company is the preferable format (see Chapter 7). Under the 2002 Commonhold and Leasehold Reform Act, the nominee purchaser is replaced by a 'Right To Enfranchise' (RTE) company, but this provision is not in force at the time of publication. A solicitor will be able to advise you on the mechanics of setting up an appropriate type of company.

It is possible to withdraw a notice to buy the freehold at any time before a contract is signed, but you will have to pay your landlord's costs. If you withdraw, you cannot give notice to buy the freehold for another twelve months.

Initial notice

Collective enfranchisement starts when the qualifying tenants, as a group, give 'initial' notice to the freeholder (known as the 'reversioner') and all other landlords. The service of an initial notice commits the qualifying tenants to paying the freeholder's and, if appropriate, the other landlords' reasonable costs. The notice must:

- Give details of the freehold property that you want to buy. You may want the freeholder to give you certain rights over other property owned by them, for example, rights of way. If so, you must say what these rights are.
- Show the property affected on a plan, including the property you wish to buy.
- Say that, on the date you give notice, the building satisfies the rules for enfranchisement.
- Give details of any leasehold interests you want to buy, for example, a head lease. If the freeholder is a public sector landlord or a housing association, give details of any flats that must be leased back.
- Give the price you propose to pay for the freehold, for any extra property such as gardens, and for any leasehold interests. If the parties cannot agree, a Leasehold Valuation Tribunal can deal with disputes over the terms on which you buy the freehold, including the price.
- Give the full name and address of each of the qualifying tenants, including any who are not part of the group. You must include details of each qualifying tenant's lease.

- Give the full name and address of your nominee purchaser.
- Give a date, at least two months ahead, by which the freeholder must give their counter notice.

Once initial notice has been given, your landlord or someone acting on your landlord's behalf may visit a flat, at any reasonable time, to value the landlord's interest. Your landlord must give ten days notice before doing this. If a landlord had agreed to sell the freehold before the initial notice was served, and the flat owners were on the point of deciding to enfranchise, they have a choice. They can either exercise their 'right of first refusal' under the 1987 Act (see Chapter 4), or proceed with the 1993 Act's provisions. It may be more straightforward to purchase under the 1987 Act, but professional advice should be obtained first.

Counter notice

The 'reversioner' must give a 'counter' notice to the nominee purchaser by the date given in the initial notice. In the counter notice, the reversioner must do one of these things:

- Agree there is a right to enfranchise and either accept the terms, or suggest different terms. If there are any flats or other property within the building that the freeholder has the right to leaseback and wants to do so, these must be mentioned. If the freeholder does not wish to leaseback any or all of this property, then the nominee purchaser will have to buy it. It is possible that an unwilling freeholder may try to obstruct your application by using this provision to increase the price you will have to pay. If the freeholder is a local authority or registered housing association, then they must take a leaseback of any flats that are occupied by secure or assured tenants. Advice on leaseback is essential; or
- Give reasons for not agreeing that there is a right to enfranchise. You then have two months from the date of the counter notice to ask a court to decide whether the right to enfranchise applied when the initial notice was served. If you

are successful, the court will order the service of a new counter notice. If you fail, the enfranchisement process is at an end; or

- Say that an application to a court will be made for an order that the flat owners cannot enfranchise because they, or one of the other landlords, intends to redevelop all or most of the building. A landlord can only do this if at least two-thirds of all the residential long leases are due to expire within five years of the date the initial notice was served. The landlord must also show that, once the leases run out, substantial works to the building will be carried out, which mean that vacant possession is needed. This is likely to be infrequent because the great majority of leases are likely to have many more than five years to run.

Agreeing terms

The nominee purchaser and the reversioner are allowed time to agree the terms for buying the property. The parties must enter into a binding contract within two months of the date when terms are agreed. If terms cannot be agreed, either party may refer the dispute to a local Leasehold Valuation Tribunal. If a reversioner does not comply with a time limit, flat owners may apply to a county court to order them to do so.

What about parts of the building not let to qualifying tenants?

Under collective enfranchisement, you buy the freehold of your block or building. You do not have the right to buy the leases of the flats or other units in the building which are not let to qualifying tenants. This includes shops, offices and flats let on short leases. The freeholder must take a leaseback of certain flats and can choose to do so in other cases.

If your freeholder is a public sector landlord, such as a local authority, it must take a leaseback of the flats it lets directly to secure tenants. If your freeholder is a registered social landlord (as are most housing associations) and has let a flat to someone other than a secure or qualifying tenant, it must also take a leaseback of that flat. Leaseback means a lease of 999 years at a peppercorn (ie zero) rent. If such leasebacks are taken, the price paid for the freehold will be reduced by the value of the leasebacks.

Any other freeholder may choose to take a leaseback of the flats or units not let to qualifying tenants. If your landlord decides not to take a leaseback of some or all of such flats or units, the nominee purchaser will have to buy them and prepare to be the new landlord of the shops or rented flats in the building after enfranchisement. Some landlords have used this provision to increase the costs of enfranchisement in the hope that it will cause the flat owners to withdraw from the purchase. Of course, you can always sell such leases subsequently.

Timetable

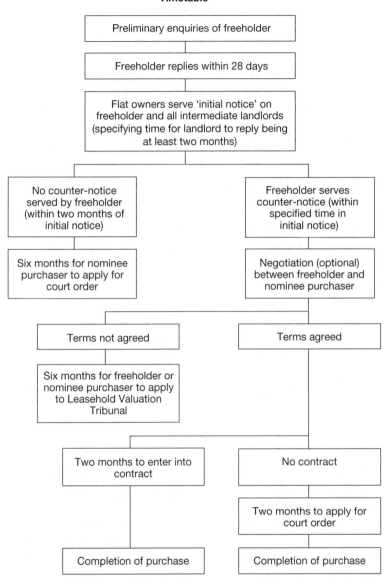

Preliminary enquiries of freeholder

Freeholder replies within 28 days

Flat owners serve 'initial notice' on freeholder and all intermediate landlords (specifying time for landlord to reply being at least two months)

No counter-notice served by freeholder (within two months of initial notice)

Freeholder serves counter-notice (within specified time in initial notice)

Six months for nominee purchaser to apply for court order

Negotiation (optional) between freeholder and nominee purchaser

Terms not agreed

Terms agreed

Six months for freeholder or nominee purchaser to apply to Leasehold Valuation Tribunal

Two months to enter into contract

No contract

Two months to apply for court order

Completion of purchase

Completion of purchase

Estate management schemes

Your building may be within the area of an estate management scheme. A scheme is set up in an area where properties are let by the same landlord who wishes to retain some powers of management over the properties. The aim is usually to ensure that the appearance and quality of an area as a whole is kept to the same standard. But a scheme can also provide for the upkeep of communal gardens or other common areas. Estate management schemes have to be approved by a Leasehold Valuation Tribunal. A scheme may:

- make provision for regulating the redevelopment, use or appearance of property
- permit the landlord to maintain, repair or renew such property
- impose obligations to maintain, repair or renew on those occupying such property; and
- permit inspections of the property.

If your building is covered by an estate management scheme, you can still go ahead with enfranchisement. But, after enfranchisement, your building will come under the rules of the scheme. If an application has been made for a scheme, you must wait until it has been approved, withdrawn or rejected. It does not matter whether the application is made before or after you give your initial notice.

Getting organised

A substantial amount of work needs to be done by, or on behalf of, the residents if the purchase of the freehold or the landlord's interest under either the 1993 Act or the 1987 Act (see Chapter 4) procedures is to be successful. Time pressure is usually not too significant, although an offer of the right of first refusal under the 1987 Act may come out of the blue. But there is a need to prepare thoroughly.

In simple terms, the tasks that need to be undertaken include:

- checking eligibility
- organising for the purchase
- choosing and instructing professional advisers
- assessing the price
- establishing the finance and funding
- dealing with the future management structure, including selecting a nominee purchaser or nominated person under the 1987 Act
- gathering information
- initial preparations
- preparing for the subsequent process.

Each step need not necessarily be in this order and, in practice, several will run together. It is important, however, that each is carried out and that no significant issue is neglected. It is also essential that you commit yourselves to the process. In many cases, a clear and binding agreement between yourselves and the nominee purchaser/nominated person – to cover how you are going to share the cost of buying the freehold and meet the professional fees – should be entered into before you start the procedure. It should be remembered that each participant's flat will increase in value, sometimes substantially, particularly if extended leases are granted at peppercorn rents after the purchase has been completed.

Once the initial notice or offer has been served, the process is up and running and you will be subject to demands for information and to deadlines. A default at any stage could endanger the process. At a certain stage in either of the two processes, you will become liable for your landlord's professional fees and costs. Nevertheless, the procedures are relatively simple, although cumbersome, and there is no reason why any group of tenants should not be able to successfully complete the purchase of the freehold of their block.

The costs

A decision about whether to buy the freehold of your block will often hinge on how much it will cost. Unfortunately, there is no easy way of arriving at a figure. Many purchases will take place on the basis of negotiation. The price paid will vary widely but is unlikely ever to be trivial. In some circumstances, the cost may be substantial. This may happen if your flat is worth a great deal – especially true in many parts of London, if the leases are close to expiring or if there are non-residential premises, such as offices and shops, in the building, and the landlord does not take a leaseback of them. And if the maximum possible number of residents do not participate, then those who do will have to pay proportionately more.

If you cannot agree a price with your landlord, the local Leasehold Valuation Tribunal (LVT) can be asked by either party to determine one. In many cases, LVTs are rejecting the high purchase prices put forward by landlords, and fixing a price much closer to the flat owners' valuation.

There is no precise formula for working out the price, although the 1993 Act does set out a basis on which a price for enfranchisement (and for lease extensions, see Chapter 5) under it can be worked out. The price of the freehold includes three elements:

- the open market value of the building which is, for enfranchisement, the value of the interests held by all the landlords in the property, assuming the flat owners are not in the market to buy
- half the 'marriage value'
- in some cases, additional compensation to a freeholder for other losses, for example, the loss of development rights following transfer of the freehold.

The value of the interest(s) is, roughly speaking, what a third party would pay if the tenants stayed in the property. It reflects the value of the rents over the years left to run on the leases, the

Buying your building under the 1993 Act   91

landlord's commissions (if any) and the value of the freehold. This is often a comparatively small sum, particularly if there are many years left to run on the lease.

Example

Take a 70 year leasehold flat worth £110,000. The landlord's freehold interest may be worth only £500 to a third party buyer. But once the freehold is bought, the property could be worth £125,000, giving a marriage value of £15,000. The flat owner will have to pay the freeholder half of this sum in addition.

Marriage value is the extra value brought about when the freehold and leasehold interests are combined and brought under the same control. These interests are often worth more together than apart and can often be the most substantial part of the price; particularly if all or most of the residential leases have only short or medium terms left to run before expiry. Marriage value is disregarded in respect of leases with an unexpired term of more than 80 years.

The table indicates the total price that might be paid when purchasing the freehold of a block in which each flat is worth £100,000. It is intended as a guide only. The figures are different in every case, and you cannot apply the figures to your situation, but you can see the kind of calculation that will be carried out. It is apparent that the longer the lease, the lower the price for that flat. A total price of the freehold is obtained by adding together the figures for each of the flats. There are other parts of a block of flats that can add to the price, such as storage areas. The block may also contain units or flats that are not held on leases by flat owners who are qualifying tenants.

If the freeholder decides not to take a leaseback of these properties, then the participating flat owners will have to purchase them, which will consequently increase the cost of enfranchisement. The last component is in respect of other losses suffered by the freeholder as a result of having to sell the freehold. This may include redevelopment potential and increased running costs, if the freeholder owns other properties and economies of scale are lost. But in most cases, this will not be significant and will rarely be an item of claim at all.

The 'right of first refusal' procedure has no similar provisions to the above (see Chapter 4), which is why a purchase under it may be cheaper than one under the 1993 Act, because it does not include marriage value.

Illustrative example

Price payable per flat for different length leases for the purchase of the freehold

Years left on lease	Marriage value (£)	50 per cent to freeholder (£)	+	Freehold value (£)	=	Payable to freeholder (£)
40	37,000	18,500	+	8,000	=	26,500
50	20,000	10,000	+	5,000	=	15,000
60	7,000	3,500	+	3,000	=	6,500
70	3,000	1,500	+	2,500	=	4,000
80	1,000	500	+	2,000	=	2,500
90	0	0	+	1,500	=	1,500

Assumptions

Example is based on a flat worth £100,000; £100 per annum ground rent; interest rate seven per cent. Freehold value includes value of ground rent income and value of reversion to freeholder. It is not practical to show the calculations involved in this illustrative example.

Examples

Two flat owners in North West London with leases of 67 years, bought the freehold of the property for a total of £67,650, a cost of £33,825 each.

Six flat owners in Hounslow, West London, with 91 year leases, bought the freehold of their block for a price of £7,075 each.

It cost four flat owners in Cardiff £5,800 each to buy their freehold.

In addition to the cost of purchasing the freehold interest, flat owners will also have to pay their own and, usually, their landlord's professional fees – for solicitors, valuers and surveyors.

Buying your building under the 1987 Act

4

Introduction

Under the 1987 Landlord and Tenant Act, qualifying tenants were given the opportunity – the 'Right of First Refusal' – to collectively buy their landlord's interest in their building or block, but only if their landlord wanted to sell. Qualifying tenants were also given a right to require a new landlord to sell to them if their right of first refusal had been ignored. These rights were subsequently amended by both the 1988 Housing Act and the 1993 Leasehold Reform, Housing and Urban Development Act (the 1993 Act); and were further strengthened by the 1996 Housing Act. In particular, it is now a criminal offence if a landlord fails to do what the law requires.

Even if the residents do not wish to buy their landlord's interest, the 1987 Act's procedures allow them to delay the process for a minimum of four months without penalty. Such a delay might be sufficient to persuade a potential buyer, of whom the residents do not approve, to abandon their proposed purchase.

There is a fundamental difference between 'collective enfranchisement' under the 1993 Act (see Chapter 3) and the Right of First Refusal. The first allows tenants to take the initiative, and permits them to buy the freehold compulsorily when they wish to do so. By contrast, the second leaves the initiative with their landlord. But if their landlord wishes to sell, which they are not obliged to do, they must offer the property to their tenants at the same price as they are seeking elsewhere.

Another disadvantage of the Right of First Refusal is that if what the tenants' immediate landlord has to sell is a lease, that is all the tenants will have the opportunity to buy. They do not have the right to buy the freehold if their landlord is not the freehold owner.

Although the Right of First Refusal has – for most flat owners at least – been largely superseded by the 1993 legislation, and now by the new 'Right to Manage' (see Chapter 6, page 130) it is not entirely obsolete, or of little or no potential value. For example, a purchase under the Right of First Refusal is sometimes possible when it is not available under the 1993 Act. This is because more residents are eligible and there are less severe restrictions relating to the existence of shops and offices in a building. In addition, a purchase under the 1987 Act can be cheaper than one under the 1993 Act. The reason for this is that under the 1987 Act, the price does not include 'marriage value' (see Chapter 3). The other benefits and drawbacks of a purchase under the Right of First Refusal are similar to those for 'collective enfranchisement' although it would not be possible in many cases for the new owners to grant themselves extended leases.

This chapter explores:

- The Right of First Refusal under the 1987 Landlord and Tenant Act.
- The standard process and disposal by auction.
- How the right can be lost.
- What if the property is sold without the residents having first refusal?

At the end of the chapter, a table illustrates the principal differences between the Right of First Refusal and collective enfranchisement. Chapter 3 covers tenant's right to buy the freehold of their building, which is available to flat owners collectively.

Which tenants qualify?

Most occupiers qualify for the Right of First Refusal, including flat owners and regulated tenants, but not assured tenants, protected shorthold tenants, and most business and service tenants. Flat owners are excluded if they own three or more flats in the building. A subtenant only qualifies if their landlord is not a qualifying tenant.

More people can qualify for the Right of First Refusal than for collective enfranchisement. It would however often be a more effective and always a less expensive solution, if a large number of the residents of a building are tenants rather than flat owners, to pursue the option of applying to a court for the appointment of a manager (see Chapter 6). Another option is the new Right to Manage, which does not require flat owners to prove that their manager is at fault, or to pay a premium (see Chapter 6).

Which properties?

The Right of First Refusal applies to the disposal of any property not just a purpose-built block containing two or more flats held by qualifying tenants, provided that more than 50 per cent of the flats in the property being sold are held by qualifying tenants.

If the building is used partly for non-residential purposes, such as shops or offices, flat owners and tenants will be excluded from the Right of First Refusal if more than 50 per cent of the floor space, disregarding common parts, is used for non-residential purposes.

Example

A building is made up of a ground floor shop with nine flats above. Two of the flats are vacant; six are owned by long leaseholders and one is let to a protected shorthold tenant. The six leaseholders are all qualifying tenants. As over 50 per cent of the flats are owned by qualifying tenants and as more than 50 per cent of the floor space is used for residential purposes, they have a right of first refusal if the landlord decides to sell his or her interest.

In addition, buildings whose landlords are local authorities, housing associations, or other public sector landlords, are excluded from the 1987 Act. A building that has a resident landlord is also excluded. A resident landlord is defined as a landlord who has lived in a flat in the building as their only, or main home, for at least a year at the time they wish to sell their interest in the property. However, a landlord does not count as a resident landlord if the building was originally constructed as a block of flats. There are special rules when there is a chain of landlords and the immediate landlord of the tenants of the flats has a leasehold interest of less than seven years, or there is an option allowing the superior landlord to terminate the lease within the first seven years. All other landlords are subject to the Right of First Refusal.

Which sales are affected?

Most sales or other transfers of a landlord's interest in a building, known as a 'relevant disposal', are caught by the 1987 Act. A relevant disposal takes place when a contract is entered into. If a landlord enters into a contract with another person, before the Right of First Refusal procedure is started, then the landlord commits a criminal offence. Certain non-commercial transactions are allowed to go ahead without the flat owners and tenants being entitled to exercise the Right of First Refusal. These include: gifts to members of a landlord's family; disposals to a charity; transfers to a landlord's heirs if the landlord dies; bankruptcy; and transfers under a Compulsory Purchase Order.

The Right of First Refusal does not apply if a landlord is selling the lease of a single flat in the building, or if the landlord is a company and it transfers its interest to another company within the same group of companies, provided that company has been associated with the landlord for at least two years. It is also likely that the Right of First Refusal does not arise if the landlord is a company and its interest in the property is indirectly sold by a purchaser buying shares in the company which owns the property, rather than the property itself.

The standard process

If a landlord wishes to sell their interest in the property, they must first offer to sell it to the resident qualifying tenants. The procedure is outlined below.

Landlord's offer to sell

The landlord must serve a written notice which the 1987 Act calls a 'Section 5', or offer notice. It should include details of the interest being sold, the terms of the sale and the price, and offer to sell on those terms. This offer must remain open for acceptance for at least two months ('the acceptance period'). The landlord must allow a further period of at least two months for a person, or persons, to be chosen by the qualifying tenants to buy the landlord's interest on their behalf ('the nomination period').

The notice must be served on not less than 90 per cent of the qualifying tenants; or, if there are less than ten, on all but one of them. The fact that you might not have been served with the notice does not prevent you from joining the other qualifying tenants in accepting the offer, or making a counter offer.

Tenants' response

If you are interested in buying the landlord's interest (or in delaying the sale), the other qualifying tenants should be contacted as soon as possible, in order to discuss and decide what action to take. One possibility would be to call a meeting to canvass opinion. The other residents must be contacted because a majority – over 50 per cent – of those qualifying for the Right of First Refusal must be in favour either of accepting the landlord's offer, or of putting forward a counter offer for the process to proceed. If there are joint tenants or joint flat owners, then they have one vote between them rather than one vote each. Swiftness in reaching a decision is important because your landlord may only have held the offer open for the minimum period of two months.

What happens if the offer is not accepted and there is no counter offer?

If a majority of qualifying tenants do not accept your landlord's offer or put forward a counter offer within the period allowed in the offer notice, the landlord is free to sell to whomever they like within the following 12 months without making a further offer. However, the sale must be on the same terms and at a price at least as high as that originally offered to you. If not, a criminal offence is committed.

Who is to buy the property?

If you accept an offer, you have a further period of at least two months from the end of the initial period to get organised. You will need to sort out the financial arrangements. You will also need to agree who is to buy the property on the participants' behalf – known as the 'nominated person'. The nominated person could be a company set up by the participants, one or more (up to four) individual tenants, an association or some third party. In most situations, a company is the best option. In effect, the nominated person will become the new landlord once the purchase has been completed.

Should a counter offer be made?

If there are enough people interested in buying, you should always consider making a counter offer to your landlord's offer. This means asking the landlord to accept a lower price for their interest in the property than the price included in the offer notice. There are two reasons for this.

First, if your landlord is anxious to sell without delay, they may have no alternative but to sell to the qualifying tenants. The 1987 Act does not allow a landlord to sell to anyone else for a minimum period of two months from the date of the offer notice. A landlord might be prepared to accept a lower offer for the property, to get the sale completed quickly.

Second, even if your landlord rejects the counter offer, they will not be able to sell to a third party at a price lower than that in their offer notice. If you have reason to believe that your landlord's asking price is higher than the 'going rate' for their interest in the property, then you should have the property professionally valued. If the valuation is lower than the offer price, you may be successful in persuading your landlord to accept it.

A Leasehold Valuation Tribunal has no power to deal with disputes over the terms on which a landlord's interest is bought under this procedure, including the price.

What happens when a counter offer is made?

If you make a counter offer, your landlord can respond in one of three ways:

- The landlord can reject the counter offer without putting forward a fresh offer. In that case, the landlord will be free to sell to whomever they choose during the following 12 months without having to make a further offer to the qualifying tenants. However, the sale must be on the same terms and at a price at least as high as the offer to the qualifying tenants; or

- The landlord can reject the counter offer but continue negotiations by making a fresh offer to the qualifying tenants. If the negotiations are successful and a sale is agreed, the process will continue in the same way as if the landlord's first offer had been accepted. If the negotiations break down, the position will be the same as if the landlord rejected the counter offer without putting forward a fresh offer; or

- The landlord can accept the counter offer. In this case, the process will continue in the same way as if the qualifying tenants had accepted the landlord's first offer.

How is an offer accepted or a counter offer made?

If a majority of qualifying tenants wish to either accept their landlord's offer, or to make a counter offer, they must serve a written notice to this effect within the period allowed by the landlord in the offer notice. The notice must specify the names of all the people accepting the offer, or making the counter offer, and the addresses of their flats. If a counter offer is being made, the notice must also set out the terms, including the price, on which the qualifying tenants are prepared to buy the property.

What happens if an offer or a counter offer is accepted?

Once a landlord's offer, or the qualifying tenants' counter offer, is accepted then, until the end of the period allowed by the landlord for a purchaser to be chosen (at least four months from when the offer notice was served), the landlord is not allowed to sell their interest to anyone except the nominated person chosen by the qualifying tenants to buy the property on their behalf.

This period of restriction on a landlord's freedom to sell is extended by a further three months if a purchaser is actually selected by a majority of qualifying tenants within the time allowed by the landlord for a purchaser to be chosen.

If a purchaser is not chosen within the time allowed after agreeing a sale, a landlord is free to sell to whomever they like within the following 12 months without making a further offer to the qualifying tenants. The sale must be on the same terms and at a price at least as high as offered to the qualifying tenants.

Withdrawal from the sale

The fact that a sale has been agreed by the acceptance of an offer, or counter offer, does not in itself commit the qualifying tenants or the landlord to proceed with the sale. This is because offers and counter offers are made 'subject to contract'; on the basis that no binding commitment to the sale has been made before a formal contract has been agreed. Once a formal contract has been agreed, it will not usually be possible for one party to withdraw from the sale without the other's consent. Before this, either party can withdraw at any time.

The landlord withdraws

Withdrawal by a landlord will be in one of the following situations:

- The property has ceased to be covered by the 1987 Act. This could happen if, for example, a flat in the building becomes vacant after the offer notice has been served, causing the number of flats let to qualifying tenants to be less than half of the total number of flats. In this situation, a landlord can withdraw from the sale and will be free to sell their interest without first giving the qualifying tenants an opportunity to buy. You should seek advice if your landlord claims this situation applies. Each party will have to pay its own legal fees in connection with the sale.

- The property is still covered by the Act but a landlord withdraws prior to the qualifying tenants selecting a purchaser. In this situation, the landlord is not entitled to sell their interest in the property without making a fresh offer. Each party will have to pay its own legal fees in connection with the sale.

- The property is still covered by the Act but a landlord withdraws after a purchaser has been selected but within three months of the passing of the deadline for choosing a purchaser. In this case, the landlord is not entitled to sell their interest in the property without making a fresh offer to the qualifying tenants. If the landlord withdraws more than four weeks after the start of the period allowed for a purchaser to be selected, they would have to pay the purchaser's legal costs from the end of the four weeks to the time of withdrawal. Otherwise, each party will have to pay its own legal fees in connection with the sale.

- The property is still covered by the Act but a landlord withdraws after a purchaser has been selected, but more than three months after the deadline for choosing a purchaser has passed. In this situation, the landlord is free to sell their interest to whoever they choose within the following 12 months. As before, the sale must be on the same terms and at a price at least as high as offered to the qualifying tenants. The landlord is entitled to their legal costs from the end of the four-week period to the date of withdrawal. The person or persons chosen to be the purchaser, together with the qualifying tenants who agreed to the sale, will be 'jointly and severally' bound to pay the landlord's legal costs.

The tenants withdraw

This depends on when withdrawal takes place. Once a purchaser has been chosen, the qualifying tenants must withdraw by the nominated person serving a notice on the landlord to this effect. A withdrawal notice must be served if there is no longer a majority of qualifying tenants who wish to proceed with the purchase.

- You withdraw after the offer, or counter offer, has been accepted, but before choosing a purchaser. Before the deadline for choosing a purchaser, a landlord is not allowed to sell their interest without making a further offer. Once the deadline has passed, a landlord is free to sell to whomever they choose within the following 12 months. Again, the sale must be on the same terms and at a price at least as high as offered to the qualifying tenants. Each party will have to pay its own legal costs in connection with the sale.

- You withdraw after choosing a purchaser. In this situation, a landlord is free to sell to whomever they choose within the following 12 months, without making a further offer. Again, the sale must be on the same terms and at a price at least as high as offered to the qualifying tenants. If the qualifying tenants withdraw more than four weeks after the start of the period allowed by the landlord for a purchaser to be chosen, then together with the person, or persons, chosen to be the purchaser, they are 'jointly and severally' liable for the landlord's legal costs from the end of the four weeks to the time of withdrawal. Otherwise, each side pays its own legal costs in connection with the sale.

Disposal by auction

This is a procedure to allow landlords to obtain the market price for their property. It works by allowing the nominated person to take the place of the successful bidder at an auction. Again, there are elaborate rules to be followed, similar in most respects to the standard process, although the time limits are often shorter. The nominated person has to accept the terms of the contract, including the price, and fulfil any conditions, such as to pay a deposit, agreed by the successful bidder at the auction.

Can the Right of First Refusal be lost?

The 1987 Act has a procedure under which a prospective purchaser of the landlord's interest can seek to ensure that the Right of First Refusal is lost. A prospective purchaser must first serve a notice on at least 80 per cent of the tenants of the premises they wish to buy, which informs them of the terms and price of the proposed sale. The flat owners and tenants do not have to be qualifying tenants. The prospective purchaser's notice must invite the flat owner or tenant to serve a notice on them. This notice should ask whether the landlord has offered first refusal and, if the landlord has not, whether the flat owner or tenant knows of any reason why they might not be entitled to the right, and whether they would like to exercise it. The prospective purchaser's notice must also warn the recipient how this procedure can lead to the Right of First Refusal being lost.

Unless at least 50 per cent of the flat owners and tenants served with the prospective purchaser's notice respond within two months then the Right of First Refusal is lost. It is also lost if more than 50 per cent of the flat owners and tenants served do respond within the time limit, but they all say either that they do not think they are entitled to the right, or they do not wish to exercise it.

Once the Right of First Refusal has been lost in this way, the prospective purchaser may safely buy the landlord's interest without first having to wait for the landlord to go through the process of offering their interest to the qualifying tenants.

The purchaser also avoids the risk of the qualifying tenants subsequently pointing to a failure by the landlord to comply with the procedures laid down by the Act.

If you receive a notice from a prospective purchaser, you should contact the other residents without delay and discuss what you intend to do. If the prospective purchaser is told that you wish to exercise your Right of First Refusal this does not commit you in any way. The next step would be for your landlord to serve offer notices on the qualifying tenants under the standard first refusal procedure.

What if the property is sold without the residents having first refusal?

If your landlord sells their interest in your building to a new landlord without first offering it to you, the new landlord can be ordered to re-sell it to you. If the requisite majority of residents discover that the property has been sold without their having had an opportunity to buy it, they can ask the new landlord for information about the terms of the sale. This is important because in some circumstances, the new landlord is entitled to receive the same amount that they paid the old landlord. You will usually discover that the property has been sold when the new owner informs you of their name and address. Failure to do this is a criminal offence. If you have not been told the name and address of your new landlord, you have rights to obtain this information (see Chapter 6).

You have four months from the discovery of the sale to serve a notice requesting the information about the terms of the sale. The new landlord has one month to reply. You can serve a 'purchase notice' on the new landlord within six months of their response or, if no notice is served requesting the information, within six months of your discovery of the sale. If your new landlord fails to sell to you, a court can order them to do so.

Residents have similar rights in respect of any subsequent disposals. Disputes about the terms and valuation in these circumstances can be referred to a Leasehold Valuation Tribunal.

The principal differences between the Right of First Refusal and Collective Enfranchisement		
	Right of First Refusal	Collective Enfranchisement
Residential status	Flat owners & regulated tenants	Flat owners
Resident landlords	Does not apply if flat in a converted block, occupied as only or main residence for 12 months	Same conditions, but only if block contains no more than four flats. A relative can occupy
Exempt landlords	Crown, local authorities, registered housing associations and most other public authorities	Crown (may voluntarily agree), charitable housing trusts (if flat provided for charitable purposes)
Subletting	Subtenant of qualifying tenant has no right, even if also qualifying	Tenant at end of a subletting chain has statutory right, even if their landlord would qualify
Non-residential use	Does not apply if over 50 per cent of block has non-residential use	Does not apply if over 25 per cent of block has non-residential use
'Trigger'	Only on relevant disposal by landlord	At any time
Covered in this guide in	Chapter 4	Chapter 3

This table was derived originally from Trevor M. Aldridge's book, *The Law of Flats* published by Longman, 1994.

Extending your lease 5

Introduction

All leases come to an end sometime. A defining feature of a
leasehold is that it is granted for a limited period. All leases, when
drafted, set out the length of the term of years agreed and its
starting date. The exact date of expiry, if not explicitly stated, can
easily be determined. When the lease expires, the contractual
relationship between landlord and flat owner ends. The lease
terminates at the end of the period without either party having to
do anything.

While a lease has many years to run, the flat will be easily saleable
and the prospect of homelessness is a distant possibility for
most flat owners. The problem emerges towards the end of a
long lease, when a flat owner must face the imminent likelihood
of losing their home, and perhaps an expensive claim for any
dilapidation (ie disrepair) to put the flat back into good repair.
Flats with only a short term left on the lease are hard to sell or, at
least, hard to sell at a good price. Mortgage finance is difficult,
sometimes impossible, to obtain when a lease has 30 years or
less to run, and a loan is unlikely to be advanced to carry out
major repairs.

A flat owner may benefit from some statutory protection when the
lease ends (see Chapter 1), and can usually remain in occupation.
In most cases, this is as an assured tenant paying a market rent.
This is, of course, not as good as a new long lease but is better
than being made homeless. An astute flat owner, towards the
end of a long lease, could offer to take money in return for leaving
the flat, so that the landlord can get vacant possession of the
property. This may be a substantial sum in some cases but is

unlikely to be sufficient to buy another flat, and the flat owner may prefer to stay as an assured tenant.

An alternative is to exercise either of the rights – to purchase the freehold (known as 'collective enfranchisement') or a lease extension – contained in the 1993 Leasehold Reform, Housing and Urban Development Act. Enfranchisement is only possible if a large enough group of flat owners act together to buy the freehold, so it may not be a practicable option (see Chapter 3). The right to a lease extension is an individual right, so it will usually be available even where enfranchisement is not. If you do not qualify under either of these provisions, you may be able to negotiate a new lease with your landlord. While you have the advantage of being in possession, the landlord does not have to agree.

Flat owners are entitled to exercise their right to a lease extension, provided they are 'qualifying tenants'. There is no need to wait until the lease expires; a lease extension can be purchased at any time. The new lease adds another 90 years to the time left to run on the existing lease. The new lease will be at a peppercorn rent, but the other terms of the new lease will be the same as the old.

This chapter looks at:

- The benefits of extending your lease.
- The lease extension provisions of the 1993 Leasehold Reform, Housing and Urban Development Act.
- Getting organised for a lease extension.
- The likely costs of a lease extension.
- The links with collective enfranchisement.

The benefits of extending your lease

Why should a flat owner go to the trouble and expense of extending their lease? After all, they will still have the same landlord, albeit with a longer lease to their flat after the process is completed. There are a number of identifiable advantages, and some disadvantages, which you should consider before coming to a decision:

- The right to a lease extension is an individual right – you do not have to act collectively with the other residents.

- Since a lease extension can be bought individually, there are no rules about majorities to be satisfied. You do not have to concern yourself with your neighbours, or whether they agree with you.

- There are fewer circumstances in which properties are exempt compared with a purchase of the freehold, so you may qualify for an extension, even if you do not qualify for enfranchisement.

- There may be insufficient qualifying tenants in a block interested in collective enfranchisement.

- The administrative complexity of the collective enfranchisement process may discourage you – the lease renewal procedure is in many ways simpler.

- It is cheaper to renew your lease than to enfranchise.

- There is no need to form a flat management company.

- You may find that your flat increases in value.

There appear to be no serious disadvantages to buying a lease extension, provided the price is right. However, it does not solve any management or similar problems because your landlord remains the same as before, and you will have less freedom to run your block than a purchase of the freehold would bring.

Which tenants qualify?

To have these rights you must be a 'qualifying tenant'. Generally, the rules for a lease extension are similar to those for enfranchisement under the 1993 Act (see Chapter 3). You must have a long lease (generally one that was originally granted for more than 21 years, see page 77 above). The low rent and residence qualifications were abolished by the 2002 Commonhold and Leasehold Reform Act, which introduced a different qualification. It is now necessary for the flat owner to have been a qualifying tenant for two years before the application to extend the lease. If a person who has been a qualifying tenant for two years dies, the right to extend may be exercised by their personal representatives (executors or administrators). Unlike enfranchisement, if you own more than two flats in the building, you are not excluded from a lease extension. A resident may be a qualifying tenant for a lease extension of any number of flats in the block.

Which properties?

On the purchase of a new lease, the only property concerned is the tenant's flat, together with associated land, or premises such as a garden or garage. The characteristics of the block are not relevant. The presence in the block of rented flats, commercial property, or a resident landlord, are all immaterial. There are few property exemptions. The main exemption is where the flat owner's immediate landlord is a charitable housing trust (this includes many housing associations), and the flat forms part of the accommodation provided by the trust in connection with the charitable purposes.

The process

The procedures leading to an extended lease are similar to those for collective enfranchisement (see Chapter 3). But, given that there are only two parties involved, they are considerably simpler. Lease extension may involve an intervening landlord rather than the freeholder of the property, if such a landlord's lease is long enough: it must be more than 90 years longer than the flat owner's. A flat owner acquires a new lease either from the freeholder, or if there is an intermediate lease, from the owner of that lease, provided it is long enough to grant a new long lease. For example, if a flat owner has a lease with a remaining term of 30 years, any intermediate landlord must have a term in excess of 120 years. This is because the new lease will be for a term of 90 years plus the number of years remaining on the existing lease.

Example

Freeholder
|
Landlord A
Intermediate landlord with 180 years remaining on lease
|
Landlord B
Intermediate landlord with 90 years remaining on lease
|
Flat owner
With 25 years remaining on lease

A flat owner exercising the right to buy a new lease cannot serve notice on Landlord B because they do not have a sufficiently long enough lease to grant the flat owner a new lease of 115 years. The flat owner has to serve notice on Landlord A.

As with collective enfranchisement, a flat owner can, without obligation, serve a discovery notice on their landlord and find out exactly who owns the freehold; where their landlord is based; and, if there are any intermediate leases, obtain information about these as well. Again, there is no prior requirement to obtain a professional valuation although if you are contemplating extending your lease, you should consult a valuer early on to find out how much you might have to pay. Advice on the legal issues involved would also be advisable.

Initial notice

The process for a lease extension is similar to that for enfranchisement (see Chapter 3). A flat owner who decides to buy a new lease must serve a formal notice on the landlord. The landlord must have a lease longer than the flat owner's by more than 90 years. If there is no such landlord, then the notice should be given to the freeholder.

There is no set form for the notice, but it must give:

- your full name and the address of your flat
- a description of your flat
- details of your lease
- evidence to show you are a qualifying tenant
- proof that you satisfy the two year ownership test
- the price you propose to pay for the new lease
- full details if you think the new lease should have different terms to the old one
- the name of any agent acting for you
- a date, at least two months ahead, by which the landlord must respond
- details of other parties, if any, being served with the notice.

A copy of the notice should be sent to any other person who owns an intermediate lease above the flat owner's but below that of the landlord or freeholder to whom it is being given. Once notice has been given, your landlord, or their agent, may visit your flat at any reasonable time to value the landlord's interest. Ten days' notice of such a visit must be given.

Counter notice

Your landlord must give counter notice by the date specified in your notice. In it your landlord must:

- agree that you have a right to a new lease and either accept your terms or suggest different ones; or
- give reasons for not agreeing that you have the right to a new lease. You may, within two months of the date of the counter notice, ask a court to decide whether the right to a new lease applied when you gave your notice; or
- say if they will be applying to a court for an order that you may not have a new lease because they plan to redevelop all or most of the building. The same restrictions about this apply as to the enfranchisement process (see Chapter 3).

Situations in which a landlord can deny entitlement will be rare. If a landlord fails to respond to an application for a new lease, the flat owner has six months to apply to a court to have their proposals accepted. If a flat owner does not keep to the time limits, their application for lease renewal is treated as being withdrawn. They become liable for the landlord's reasonable costs and are prevented from making a fresh application for one year. A landlord is entitled at any time after receipt of the flat owner's notice to require the payment of a deposit. This may be ten per cent of the premium proposed in the flat owner's notice, or £250, whichever is the greater.

Agreeing terms

You have at least two months to negotiate with your landlord over the terms of the purchase. If you cannot agree, you may apply to the local Leasehold Valuation Tribunal for the terms, including the price, to be settled.

Assuming that a flat owner's entitlement to a new lease has been accepted and that any disputes over the terms or price have been resolved, then the landlord must grant a new lease.

The new lease will be for a term of 90 years plus the number of years remaining on the existing lease. No ground rent is payable for the entire lease term; it will be at a 'peppercorn'. The new lease's provisions will usually be the same as those of the existing lease. If new provisions are required or added (for example, to take account of any alterations to the flat, or to remedy a defect in the lease), they will only take effect after the termination of the flat owner's existing lease, unless otherwise agreed.

The new lease must also contain a clause giving the landlord the right to repossession of the flat for the purposes of redevelopment. This right will again not arise until the end of the term of the existing lease and is subject to a court application, and to the payment of full compensation to the flat owner for the market value of the lease.

Example

If an existing lease has 20 years to run and the flat owner obtains a new lease for 110 years, any new provisions will only take effect after 20 years; although no ground rent will be payable from the start of the new lease.

Getting organised

A substantial amount of work needs to be done by, or on behalf of, the flat owner if the purchase of a new lease is to be successful. This includes:

- checking eligibility
- choosing and instructing professional advisers
- assessing the premium
- establishing the finance
- gathering information
- initial preparations, including drawing up the notice
- preparing for the subsequent process.

The steps need not necessarily be in this order and, in practice, several will run together. It is important, however, that each is carried out and that no significant issue is neglected. Once the initial notice has been served, the process is up and running and you will be subject to demands for information, and to deadlines. A default at any stage could endanger the process. After service of the notice, you will be liable for the landlord's professional fees and expenses, whether you complete or not. Nevertheless, the procedures are straightforward, and there is no reason why you should not be able to successfully complete a lease extension application.

The costs

As with enfranchisement, a decision about obtaining a new lease will often hinge on the total costs involved. A flat owner has to pay a premium for the purchase of a new lease, together with the landlord's professional costs, including solicitor's and surveyor's fees. A flat owner can obtain advice about valuation, and valuers must assess the value of a new lease in accordance with the principles set out in the legislation. Valuation is not an exact science and it is almost impossible to calculate a single, fixed price. Usually, valuers provide a 'best' and a 'worst' figure so that a flat owner will know, in advance, the likely range within which the price will eventually be settled. As with enfranchisement, there is no precise formula for working out the price, although the 1993 Act does set out a basis on which it can be worked out.

The price of a new lease includes three elements:

- the open market value of the flat, which is the reduction in the value of the landlord's interests in your flat affected by the grant of a new lease; and
- half the 'marriage value'; and,
- in some cases compensation to a landlord for other losses.

The value of the interest(s) is, roughly speaking, what a third party would pay if the flat owners stayed in the property. It reflects the value of the rents over the years left to run on the leases, the landlord's commissions (if any), and the value of the freehold. This if often a comparatively small sum, particularly if there are many years left to run on the lease.

The value of a flat owner's interest increases when they buy a new lease, while the value of the landlord's interest falls. But there will often be an overall increase in the total value of the two interests. The difference between the total value of the interests before and after lease renewal is the 'marriage value'. This is calculated differently than it is for collective enfranchisement. Marriage value is disregarded in respect of leases with an unexpired term of more than 80 years.

Illustrative example

A lease has 60 years left to run and a ground rent of £100 a year is payable. The current value of the flat is £90,000 but with an additional 90 years lease, it will be worth £99,000. The value to the flat owner will thus increase by £9,000. In this case, the landlord's interest will be reduced by about £3,000. The marriage value will be about £6,000. The landlord is entitled to at least half of this (£3,000). In this example, the flat owner will have to pay the landlord a total of about £6,000 plus compensation, if any, and the landlord's reasonable professional fees and other expenses. It is not practical to show the assumptions or calculations involved in this illustrative example.

Flat owners buying new leases may have to obtain either a mortgage or re-mortgage of their flat. The position of mortgage lenders is safeguarded under the legislation. Any existing mortgage on the flat will be converted into a mortgage on the new lease.

The links with enfranchisement

Flat owners can apply for a lease extension before, during or after enfranchisement. Obviously, there could be problems if some flat owners wish to enfranchise while others wish to purchase a lease extension. This can only be sorted out by the individuals concerned. The legislation gives procedural priority to enfranchisement. If you apply for a lease extension during enfranchisement, the application will be frozen until the enfranchisement process has ended.

Other rights 6

Introduction

In addition to a flat owner's rights concerning service charges, to buy the freehold of their block collectively, to extend their lease and of first refusal, a flat owner has other rights and the landlord has other duties. If your landlord is difficult, there are various legal provisions available which may allow you to take them to a court or to a Leasehold Valuation Tribunal to enforce your rights. In some situations failure by a landlord to carry out a duty is a criminal offence for which a local council may prosecute.

The Secretary of State (in England) and the National Assembly for Wales have the power to approve codes of practice governing residential property management. These are statements of the law and good practice and if there is a dispute, the codes can be used as evidence of which management standards should apply. In addition, departure from the codes is now a ground for the appointment of a manager (see section on the Appointment of a manager, page 137).

The relevant code is the Service Charge Residential Management Code, approved in 1996 and published by the Royal Institution of Chartered Surveyors (RICS). This code is likely to be updated to reflect recent legislative changes, and until this happens, RICS is providing an addendum to the Code with new purchases. In addition, there is the Code of Practice for Private Retirement Housing, which relates to leases of properties designated for retired people (essentially private sheltered housing), which has been approved in England, and is under consideration in Wales (available from the Association of Retirement Housing Managers).

This chapter explains these main additional rights. They are:

- The right to information about your landlord.
- The right to seek recognition of a tenants' association.
- Rights about insurance.
- The right to be consulted about the appointment of a managing agent.
- Rights over repairs.
- The right to seek the appointment of a manager.
- The right of compulsory acquisition of the landlord's interest in the block.
- Rights about permissions.
- Limits on administration charges.

Your rights in connection with service charges, major works and management audits are dealt with in Chapter 2.

Information about your landlord

It has long been a concern that tenants should know who their landlord is. It is crucial to have this information, because most of the rights described elsewhere in this guide would be of little value in practice if your landlord cannot be identified or found. Various legal provisions – principally found in the 1985 and 1987 Landlord and Tenant Acts – have been introduced with limited success. The result has been further legislation, and the measures now overlap each other to some extent.

Who is your landlord?

The tenant of a flat has a right to know the identity of their landlord. A written request can be made to the person who demands the rent, or who last received it, or who acts as the landlord's agent. The recipient then has 21 days in which to supply a written statement giving the landlord's name and address. Failure to do so without good reason is a criminal offence.

If it appears that your landlord is a company, you can write again – to your landlord, the agent, or the person who demands the rent – asking to be provided with the names and addresses of the company's directors and secretary. It is an offence if, without reasonable excuse, your landlord does not give this information in writing within 21 days, or an agent or rent collector does not pass the request on to the landlord.

Address for service

By law, landlords must notify flat owners of an address in England and Wales where notices can be served, for example, in connection with court proceedings. This may be the address of a representative such as a solicitor. If a landlord fails to do this, the flat owner's obligation to pay rent and service charge is suspended.

There is an exception to this rule if an independent receiver or manager has been appointed by a court (see later). In this case, the rent and service charge are due, even if the demand does not contain the landlord's name and address.

If you do decide to withhold payment of the rent and service charge, it is wise to pay the money withheld into your bank account in order to keep it on deposit until such time as the landlord provides you with the information.

Change of landlord

When a landlord sells their interest in the property, the new landlord must inform the flat owners in writing that the sale has taken place and give their name and address. This information should be given within two months of the sale's completion, or by the next day on which rent is due, whichever is the later. Failure to do so without good reason is a criminal offence. Furthermore, until the flat owner has been given this information, the old landlord remains liable for any breaches of covenant (for example, an obligation to keep the building in a good state of repair).

Absentee or missing landlords

Sometimes landlords cannot be traced. Their identity may be known but not their current address. Sometimes the name and address of a landlord are known, but they fail to respond. If the property is registered, a search can be made at the appropriate Land Registry office and the details obtained. This does not require the landlord's consent. You can apply using a standard form available from legal stationers, or from the Land Registry, or you can do the search online using the Land Registry website. There is a small fee.

If your landlord's interest in the property has been sold recently, the Land Registry will not be able to give you the new landlord's name and address until the register has been changed. The address the Land Registry has may not be the landlord's current address because there is no obligation to notify changes of address.

It is not unknown for landlords to vanish, or to fail to respond to flat owners. This would mean that the landlord was in breach of their obligations to the flat owners. An application can be made to a Leasehold Valuation Tribunal to appoint another party, known as a manager, to act on behalf of the missing landlord (see section on the Appointment of a manager, page 137). A majority of leaseholders can subsequently – after at least two years – apply to a court to acquire the building compulsorily (see section on Compulsory acquisition, page 138). Alternatively, a court can appoint a 'receiver' to take over the landlord's duties. Similar rules apply when flat owners wish to enfranchise (see Chapter 3), or to extend their lease (see Chapter 5). Flat owners with absentee landlords will still have to pay the appropriate price for the freehold or the new lease.

An alternative option would be for the flat owners to agree to undertake some or all of the landlord's responsibilities (for example, repairing the building, collecting the service charges, insuring the property, etc). But this may not be an ideal long-term solution.

Recognised tenants' associations

Flat owners who have bought the freehold of, or their landlord's interest in, their block collectively, who thus become the landlords themselves, will of necessity have formed some sort of association (see Chapter 7). This short section is directed at flat owners who still have a traditional landlord.

This guide describes the legal rights and duties of landlords and flat owners. Some of these rights can be very effective. Others are less successful and should be strengthened. But it is almost always the case that the flat owners in a house or block can achieve far more if they act together through a tenants' association. A tenants' association can act as a 'watchdog' for the flat owners and for the other residents, if there are any. A landlord is more likely to take flat owners' views seriously if they are expressed as one voice. Although the legislation refers to tenants' associations, in situations where all or most of the residents of a block, or number of blocks, are flat owners, they may wish to call their body a 'residents' association', or conceivably a 'flat owners' association'.

There are a number of organisations which can advise you on how to set up a tenants' association, including local private residents federations, housing aid centres, law centres, local federations of private tenants. Some of these bodies have national headquarters. Relevant addresses are given in Chapter 12.

The legislation relating to long leases specifically provides a role for recognised tenants' associations and a method for an association to become recognised. A recognised tenants' association can:

- ask for a summary of the costs for which you are paying a service charge
- inspect accounts and receipts for the property
- ask to be sent a copy of the estimates, if flat owners are consulted about major works or services

- put forward names for the list of contractors to be asked to tender for major works

- ask to be consulted about the appointment or reappointment of a managing agent; and

- appoint a surveyor to advise on any matter relating to service charges.

An individual flat owner does not have all of these rights.

An association must satisfy two requirements to qualify as a recognised tenants' association.

First, it must be an association of qualifying tenants, that is tenants whose leases contain an obligation to pay a service charge, with or without other tenants. Nearly all flat owners will pay a service charge. A single tenants' association can represent several blocks covered by the same service charge arrangements.

Second, an association must be recognised. This can come about in one of two ways. A landlord can give written notice of recognition to the secretary of the association. There is no way to compel a landlord to recognise the association. If your tenants' association is refused recognition by your landlord, the second way is to apply to your local Rent Assessment Panel for a certificate of recognition. This will be granted at their discretion. Usually the certificate will be for four years, but the Panel may cancel it if recognition is no longer deemed appropriate. As a general guide, an association should represent at least 60 per cent of the flat owners. The local Rent Assessment Panel can be contacted at the same address as the Leasehold Valuation Tribunal (details are given in Chapter 13).

Insurance

Insurance is especially significant in a block of flats. Each flat owner and the landlord have a vital interest in the continuing upkeep and repair, indeed existence, of all the other parts of the building. Insurance of the building gives both the certainty and confidence that flat owners are ultimately protected from most eventualities, including damage caused by fire, flood, subsidence, etc.

Contents insurance

It is obviously desirable for a flat owner to insure their belongings, furniture, fittings and decorations against loss caused by fire, flood, damage, burglary, etc. However, this will not be covered by the lease and is each flat owner's individual responsibility.

A single policy covering the whole building is the easiest way to ensure that a block is fully insured. The proper insurance cover is the full rebuilding cost, which may differ from the market value. Building costs are constantly rising, so the amount of cover should be regularly adjusted. This could involve a professional valuation but an inexpensive alternative is a policy which index links the sum insured.

If this is not done, a flat owner might be faced with a loss of thousands of pounds.

All long leases should expressly impose an insurance obligation. Since most blocks of flats are insured under a single policy, most leases make the landlord responsible for insurance of the building. Generally speaking, the landlord takes out the insurance, while the premium is the responsibility of the flat owners under the lease. Normally, each flat owner will pay a share of the premium by way of a variable service charge in order to reimburse the landlord. Sometimes the insurance is recoverable as a separate 'insurance rent'. If a long lease fails to make satisfactory provision for the insurance of the building, and the parties to the lease cannot agree about how to amend it, either can apply to a Leasehold Valuation Tribunal for an order varying the lease (see Chapter 1). Legislation, particularly the 1985 Landlord and Tenant Act, has given flat owners a right to information about insurance. These rights are additional to any provisions in the lease relating to information.

Information about insurance

If the landlord is responsible for insurance, a flat owner or recognised tenants' association can ask the landlord or landlord's agent for a written summary of the current insurance cover. The landlord must provide this within one month. The summary should set out:

- the sum for which the property is insured
- the name of the insurer
- the risks covered in the policy.

Instead of supplying a summary, the landlord can supply a copy of the insurance policy itself.

Once you have seen the summary or a copy of the policy you have six months in which you can ask to inspect the insurance policy itself and any supporting documents, such as receipts, showing evidence of payment of premiums for the current period and for the period immediately preceding it. You are entitled to make copies of the policy and any supporting documents for a reasonable charge. The landlord must make the facility for inspection available free of charge for two months.

There are provisions covering information held by a superior landlord. In particular, if the whole or part of the information is needed from a superior landlord then the intermediate landlord is under a duty to go through a similar procedure to get it and the superior landlord is under a similar duty to provide it.

Failure without good reason to comply with these duties is a criminal offence.

Unsatisfactory insurance arrangements

Leases sometimes specify that a particular insurance company must be used, but if not, whoever is responsible for arranging insurance cover is free to choose any company. Disputes often arise when a landlord chooses a more expensive policy which does not provide better cover than most alternatives. Sometimes this is because they get a commission from the insurance company. The cost of insurance must be reasonable. But the fact that cheaper insurance can be obtained does not necessarily mean you will be able to challenge your landlord's insurance arrangements successfully.

Example

In a recent case, the five leaseholders of a small block of flats were expected to pay £1,400 annually in building insurance. The Leasehold Valuation Tribunal ruled that they were being over-charged by their landlord and should be paying no more than £500 a year. They were also awarded backdated refunds.

Unless a lease states which company should be used, or what risks or perils should be covered, and if the landlord is responsible for insurance, all the flat owners can do is argue that it is unfair and unreasonable for them to have to pay the whole of their contribution towards the premium. The procedure is the same as that adopted when challenging another element of a service charge (see Chapter 2).

If the flat owner is responsible for insuring the property but the landlord has the right to nominate the insurer, there are special grounds for challenging the arrangement. These are:

- the insurance cover available from the nominated insurer is unsatisfactory in some way; or
- the premiums are excessive.

Such a challenge may be made to a court, or more commonly to a Leasehold Valuation Tribunal, which may require the landlord to appoint another insurer, or an insurer who meets specified requirements. The landlord's right under a lease to nominate an insurer cannot be removed and he or she cannot be required to nominate a number of insurers from which the flat owner could choose.

In rare cases, flat owners have found that they must insure using the landlord's choice of insurance company. This practice is prevented by the 2002 Commonhold and Leasehold Reform Act.

Notification to insurers of possible claim

A particular difficulty that sometimes arises when landlords are responsible for the insurance of the building is that they fail to claim promptly, or fail to claim at all. Many insurance policies have strict time limits within which to make a claim. It is not possible for flat owners to make a formal claim unless they are party to the policy.

The 1987 Landlord and Tenant Act has come to the rescue of flat owners in this situation. You may write to the insurance company to tell them about a possible claim. You should also provide a brief description of the damage. This should be done within six months, or any longer period allowed by the policy. You should send the landlord a copy of the letter and remind them of their responsibility to make a prompt claim. If, despite this, the landlord still fails to claim and the insurance company refuses to pay, it may be possible to sue the landlord for damages.

Escape of water

One of the commonest causes of damage starting in one flat and damaging another is water, whether from damaged or defective plumbing, or simply an overflowing bath. Comprehensive insurance policies, subject to the inevitable exclusions, usually cover the escape of water from tanks and pipes resulting from, for example, freezing, or from defective heating systems. They rarely cover carelessness. The owner of a flat from which water escapes will often be liable for damages. It is usually possible for a flat owner to get an extension to a contents insurance policy to cover such an eventuality.

Managing agents

Landlords often employ managing agents to manage their property on their behalf. Problems can arise if a landlord appoints an incompetent, inefficient or dubious agent.

Example

The flat owners in a particular block pay an annual service charge of £800. Every time the managing agent of the block has, for example, a light bulb changed, a high charge is made but since receipts are provided, the agent is probably just on the right side of the law. The service charge in a similar block is around £300.

Often the best way to stop such practices is to change the agent. An individual flat owner has no general right to be consulted about the appointment of a managing agent of their block. However, the landlord must consult flat owners when the proposed appointment is for more than 12 months and the fee is more than £100 for any flat owner (see page 63).

A recognised tenants' association may ask the landlord to consult the association about the appointment, or reappointment, of an agent. The procedure to be followed depends on whether at the time of the association's request there is already a managing agent or not.

No managing agent

Before appointing a managing agent, the landlord has to serve the tenants' association with a notice stating:

- the proposed managing agent's name;
- which of the landlord's obligations it is proposed the agent is to carry out.

The notice must allow the association at least one month to make comments on the proposed appointment and give the name and address of a person to whom the comments can be sent. Although a landlord has to take any comments into account, they can still go ahead and appoint the agent, even if the association disagrees. The landlord has to follow this procedure each time there is a proposed change of agent.

Example

Some managing agents can be extremely incompetent or worse. Here is recent case history involving an agent based in the South of England. The block concerned is located in Essex.

- It did not tell the flat management company it was employing subsidiary companies including a builder, insurance broker and maintenance contractor and did not declare the commissions it was receiving.

- It engaged inept and unreliable and in some cases dishonest contractors.

- It ordered an expensive insurance revaluation without first providing estimates and without the flat management company's knowledge and consent.

- It did not implement the Royal Town Planning Institute's Code of Management Practice for over two years.

- An administrator falsified the flat management company's AGM minutes and refused to correct them.

- It regularly meddled with flat management company affairs which included attempting to choose its directors.

- It provided a very poor property management service including appointing the wrong contractor, failing to obtain quotations upon request, not paying contractors and utility companies and caused significant delays to necessary maintenance works.

- Its service charge collection and arrears administration service was chaotic. In one year, a third of service charges were in serious arrears and recovery action had not commenced. Later it secretly agreed with a leaseholder to collect less than the amount due which inevitably led to further arrears.

- It issued an incorrect Section 20 notice.

- It changed the electricity supplier without notice. It claimed savings of 20 per cent could be achieved but in fact the bills went up.

- It was contractually obliged to hold four meetings a year with the flat management company. Over a 15 month period only one was held.

- It did not respond to complaints.

Personal experience, 1999 to 2004, Paul Walentowicz

Existing managing agent

Within one month of receiving the association's notice, the landlord has to serve the association with a notice stating which of the landlord's obligations the agent carries out. The landlord must also give the association a reasonable period within which to comment on the performance of the agent, and whether the agent should continue to act in this capacity. Although a landlord has to take any comments into account, they can still retain the agent even if the association disagrees.

As long as the agent remains employed, the landlord should provide the association every five years with a notice specifying any changes in the landlord's obligations carried out by the agent. The landlord must give the association a reasonable period in which to comment on the agent's performance since it was last consulted. As before, the landlord has to take these comments into account, but is not bound by them.

If a landlord sells their interest in the property, the association loses its right to be consulted, unless it serves a fresh notice on the new landlord requesting consultation.

If you are dissatisfied with the way the agent manages the property, you should keep a diary or notes to back up your complaint. Complaints about an agent should be made in writing, the letters dated, and copies kept. This provides evidence to support any further action you might take. Acting together with other flat owners, or through a recognised tenants' association, you might exercise the right to enfranchise (see Chapter 3), or the right to manage (see the following section). Or, acting either with others or on your own, you might challenge the portion of the service charge attributable to poor management (see Chapter 2), although this option only deals with some past problems and does not offer a long term solution. The most effective form of pressure to remove a poor agent is likely to be that mounted by all the flat owners acting together, or through a tenants' association.

The right to manage

The right to manage was introduced by the 2002 Commonhold and Leasehold Reform Act. Flat owners can collectively take over the management of the building, and there is no need to go to court, or to prove any fault or inefficiency by the landlord. By taking over management, the flat owners get control over appointing managing agents, choosing the insurer, having an increased say in what services to have, and some control over service charges. Of course, the flat owners also get the burden of management. There may be disagreements between flat owners to be resolved, and the cost in time and money of organising all of the services and managing the building generally. The power to manage is an extremely useful one, but will not necessarily solve all problems.

To qualify, the flat owners must live in a building with at least two flats, and must have long leases (granted originally for more than

21 years), and at least two thirds of the flats must be owned by qualifying flat owners. At least half of the qualifying flat owners must participate (if not initially, by the time that a notice is sent to the landlord). If the landlord owns a lease of a flat, s/he counts as a qualifying flat owner. Some buildings are exempt, as follows:

- Where there is non-residential use in more than 25 per cent of the total floor area.
- A building converted into no more than four flats by the landlord, where the landlord or a family member has lived in one of the flats for 12 months.
- The building is made up of different freehold parts that are owned by different people (but it may still be possible to exercise the right in respect of one part, if it is divided from the other part or parts, and has its own services).
- Where the landlord is a local authority (there is a different right to manage: see page 132 below).
- Where the right to manage has been exercised previously, and the management has ceased within the previous four years.
- Where the property is already managed by a 'right to manage' company (see below).

These qualifications are similar to those that apply to enfranchisement, although there are differences.

The right to manage is exercised by the flat owners forming a 'right to manage' company (RTM company). This is a company that is limited by guarantee. The RTM company sends specified notices to those qualifying flat owners who have not already joined the company, advising them of their right to participate by becoming members of the RTM company. At least 14 days later, a different specified notice is sent to the landlord. The landlord has a period of at least a month in which to reply, by counternotice. The landlord may accept the right to manage, in which case the RTM company will take over three months later. If the landlord disputes the right, or if the landlord cannot be traced, then the RTM company can apply to the Leasehold Valuation Tribunal (LVT).

The LVT can decide whether the right to manage has been made out and make an order that the landlord must obey.

The landlord's costs are payable by the RTM company; disputes are again dealt with by the LVT.

The notices can be obtained from legal stationers or from suppliers advertising on the internet. The notices themselves, and the procedures involved, are not wholly straightforward, and flat owners running a RTM company should consider getting advice from a solicitor or surveyor with relevant expertise. If you are considering setting up a RTM company, you will face many of the issues that arise in flat management companies (see Chapter 7).

Local authority right to manage

Flat owners with local authority/council landlords have a right to manage, which is different from the right to manage explained above. The right is available not only to flat owners but also to council tenants. Those flat owners and tenants interested in the right to manage first form a Tenant Management Organisation (TMO). The TMO may be a company, or a different kind of legal structure called an industrial and provident society. It may be independent of the landlord (often called a Tenant Management Co-operative, TMC) or may be run jointly with the council or a housing association (an Estate Management Board, EMB).

The minimum size of a scheme managed by a TMO is 25 flats or houses, and there is no maximum size. A TMO may be set up to manage a building, an estate, or all council properties in a locality. There is a great deal of flexibility in the level of responsibility accepted by the TMO, and while some take over all management functions, some accept only some functions. The council is usually required to fund the TMO, at least in part. This is essential where the property managed by the TMO includes council tenancies, because the tenants pay rent to the council and do not pay a service charge.

The TMO appoints one of a number of specified agencies to assist with the right to manage process. The agency plays an important role in supporting the TMO and its members through the process that follows, which can take two or three years. The agency provides training to the members of the TMO, and assists in the negotiation of a management agreement between TMO and council. The council also has duties to assist the TMO as it is set up. A feasibility study and at least two ballots of flat owners and tenants take place, before the TMO (if successful) can take over management of the building or estate.

If you are considering setting up a TMO company, you will face many of the issues that arise in flat management companies (see Chapter 7). However, there is one important difference: a TMO should have a great deal of support from the council and the agency. The right and procedure is only summarised here, and further information is available from the National Federation of Tenant Management Organisations (NFTMO) and the Tenant Participation Advisory Service (TPAS) (see Chapter 12).

Repairs

Even the most modern and well-built properties will deteriorate if left to themselves. To keep a building in satisfactory, let alone good condition, regular maintenance is needed. A building is a complex, interdependent structure: a fault in one of its parts can lead to more serious damage in another. Something as simple as a blocked gutter can lead to considerable damp penetration if it is left uncleared. Proper maintenance requires both time and money and can, in some cases, be very expensive. Unsurprisingly, therefore, the upkeep of a building is often neglected or avoided. Disputes about repairs are common.

If a flat is subject to a lease of more than seven years, a landlord is only legally obliged to carry out those repairs that are specified in the lease. The terms of the lease should set out responsibilities for the management, including the repair of the building. For flats the most common arrangement is that the freeholder or landlord is responsible for keeping the structure of the building, including the common parts, in good repair. The flat owner is normally responsible for the internal decoration and upkeep of the flat and for paying a proportion of the landlord's costs of repairs and maintenance. Flat owners will also generally have a responsibility to look after the property well.

If you think your building needs attention, you should first inform your landlord. You can write to the landlord and/or the landlord's agents requesting that they deal with each specific item of disrepair within a set period. The letters should be dated and copies kept. If you think something is seriously wrong, you can ask a surveyor to inspect the building and prepare a report setting out the details of the works necessary, and send that to your landlord and/or the landlord's agent. It is sometimes possible to get a report without charge, for example, a dampproofing company may report on rising damp. A free report may be useful, but treat it with caution if it is not independent – a company may be more interested in selling its services than in solving your problem. If your landlord still takes no action, there are a number of different steps you can take. These are:

- Contact your local council. A council has broad statutory powers over the condition of housing. It has the power to inspect housing, and where the council officer concludes that there are hazards in the housing, it has the power to serve one of a number of different kinds of notice on your landlord. One of these is an 'improvement notice', requiring the landlord to carry out specified repairs within a reasonable time. If a notice is not complied with, the authority can do the work and charge the cost to the defaulter. Failure to comply with a notice is an offence. The chief advantage of contacting a council is that it can take action against your landlord and you may not need to commence legal proceedings yourself. The council will consider the seriousness of any hazard before deciding what action to take, and if the risk to health is not serious, it may not take any action at all. Remember that you have duties under your lease, and these will probably include a duty to carry out interior repairs and decoration. If a hazard results from your failure to repair, the council may serve a notice on you.

- Flat owners may carry out the repair themselves and deduct the cost from future rent (not the service charge). Before taking such action, your landlord must have had notice of the disrepair, the disrepair in question must be within the scope of your landlord's repairing obligations, and the landlord must have refused or failed to carry out the repair within a reasonable time. This method is likely to be appropriate only when the repairs are relatively inexpensive, given the modest sum paid by most flat owners in ground rent, and it is sensible to get legal advice before withholding rent.

- A flat owner's principal remedy against a landlord who fails to make repairs to a property, is to go to court to claim damages and/or a court order requiring that the work be done. Legal action of this sort should only be considered when the disrepair is serious. Compensatory damages can amount to thousands of pounds. A landlord who does not comply with a court order may be liable for imprisonment for contempt of court. If the landlord is a company, the court may order a director of the company to be imprisoned. These cases are not straightforward and it is usually advisable to get legal advice. If you are claiming benefits or have a low income, you may qualify for legal aid. (See Chapter 8 for more information about disputes).

- Some landlords may neglect their duties to such an extent that it is pointless for flat owners to take legal action against them over disrepair, for example, if a landlord has failed to carry out their repairing obligations for a number of years or if the landlord cannot be traced. In such a case, a court may appoint a 'receiver' to take over a landlord's duties. An alternative is to apply to a Leasehold Valuation Tribunal for the appointment of a 'manager' if your landlord persistently fails to maintain a block consisting of two or more flats (see next section).

The owner of a block of flats is also liable in law for any injury or damage caused to an occupier of a property and to third parties, such as neighbours or visitors, by the condition of that property. This liability arises if the landlord was under a duty to repair (usually under your lease), knew, or ought to have known, of the disrepair, and failed to repair within a reasonable time.

Grants and loans for repairs

If you own a property that needs repairs you might be able to get help from your local council to meet all or part of the cost of the work. The following are among the types of assistance which might be available:

- House renovation or repairs grant or loan – for the improvement and/or repair of houses and flats.

- Common parts grant or loan – for the improvement and/or repair of the common parts of buildings containing one or more flats.

There are important qualifying conditions – which vary council by council – and applicants are usually subject to a means test to determine eligibility for assistance. If you are in receipt of a means-tested benefit or on a very low income you could well qualify for help. Landlords can also apply for assistance in limited circumstances. If you are considering applying for help, you should contact the appropriate department of your local council for further details before any work is started. Many councils also run agencies offering help with repairs such as providing lists of approved contractors or advising about sources of finance.

If you cannot obtain assistance from your council, you may be able to get a loan or additional loan from your mortgage lender. This information about loans and grants from your council applies both to repairs or improvements that you plan to carry out yourself, and to your contribution to service charge bills if the work has not yet been carried out.

Appointment of a manager

If a building contains two or more flats, any flat owner can apply to a Leasehold Valuation Tribunal to appoint a manager to run the block, or to carry out certain management functions under provisions in the 1987 Landlord and Tenant Act. The objective is to appoint someone to take the landlord's place to organise the work and collect payments for it.

Example

The flat owners of a block of flats in Notting Hill, London won their application to appoint a manager of their choice at a Leasehold Valuation Tribunal hearing. The order removed all powers from the landlord, who is now limited to receiving the ground rents. In addition to other poor or bad practices, the trigger was the landlord's behaviour over major works to the property. The owners were not sent estimates for the works – costing almost £7,000 per flat – and, since the works began almost immediately, had no opportunity to comment on the choice of contractor or the proposed works.

An individual flat owner may make the application but in many cases all or most of the flat owners may wish to act jointly. It is advisable to seek legal advice before embarking on this course. The grounds for seeking the appointment of a manager are:

- the landlord is in breach of their obligations to you as a leaseholder; or
- the landlord has demanded, or is likely to demand unreasonable service charges; or
- the landlord has failed to comply with any relevant provision of a government approved code of management practice (see page 117).

Flat owners do not have this right if:

- their landlord is resident and you live in a converted building, unless more than half of the flats in the building are owned by other flat owners; or
- their landlord is a public body such as a local authority or a registered social landlord (most housing associations are registered social landlords); or
- the premises are included within the functional land of a charity.

The procedure

A preliminary notice must first be served on your landlord inviting them to put right any problems, if this is possible within a reasonable time. In certain circumstances, this requirement may be dispensed with. If your landlord does not put the problems right within a reasonable time, the next step is to apply for the appointment of a manager. The application should give the name and address of everyone likely to be affected by the application. It should also give the name, address and qualifications of the person the flat owners wish to act as manager. This is often a managing agent or a surveyor, but could be a company formed by the flat owners to manage the block on their behalf. In all cases, a manager will only be appointed if it is just and convenient to do so.

Compulsory acquisition

As a last resort, again under provisions in the 1987 Landlord and Tenant Act, a majority of the flat owners in a block can ask a court (not a Leasehold Valuation Tribunal) to order the landlord to transfer their interest in the property to them. It is again advisable to seek legal advice before embarking on this course. The grounds for such an order are:

- the landlord is in breach of any obligation under the applicants' leases in relation to the repair, maintenance, insurance or management of the building, and the breach is likely to continue; or

- an order for the appointment of a manager of the building has been in force for at least two years.

The first of these grounds is for use in extreme cases where the appointment of a manager would be an insufficient remedy. This might be the case if, for example, the landlord cannot be traced. Again the building in question must contain two or more flats having the same landlord.

Flat owners do not have this right if:

- their landlord is resident and you live in a converted building; or
- their landlord is a public body such as a local authority or a registered social landlord (most housing associations are registered social landlords); or
- the premises are included within the functional land of a charity; or
- more than 50 per cent of the internal floor area of the building is used for non-residential purposes; or
- the total number of flats held by qualifying leaseholders is less than two-thirds of the total number of flats contained in the building.

A preliminary notice normally needs to be served on the landlord. An acquisition order cannot be made unless the court considers it appropriate to do so in the circumstances. The terms of the order are agreed between the landlord and the flat owners, or if they cannot agree, either party can refer them to a Leasehold Valuation Tribunal. The price is likely to be what the premises would fetch on the open market. The procedure for a compulsory acquisition is similar to that for the right of first refusal (see Chapter 4).

Permissions

There are some things that your lease says you cannot do without the landlord's permission. The most common of these are subletting and alterations. If you go ahead without permission, you will have broken the terms of your lease. You may find that the landlord makes you ask your tenant to leave, or undo all of the alterations to your flat. The landlord may also serve a termination notice on you, and you may get in trouble with your mortgage lender, and end up having to pay the landlord's costs. It is important that you consider your lease before subletting or carrying out alterations.

If the landlord accepts, ask for written permission. If it is 'agreed in principle', or 'subject to licence', then the landlord will probably want you to sign a formal document prepared by the landlord's solicitor and called a 'licence', and to pay the cost of the licence. Strictly speaking, you should wait until the licence is finalised, but it is common for flat owners to go ahead relying on 'agreement in principle'.

If you have to pay fees or costs to the landlord or their agents, these are administration charges. See the end of this chapter for limits on these.

Subletting

This can include any arrangement where a person is paying you rent and living in your flat. Some leases allow 'sharing possession' or 'letting of part', which will allow you to have a lodger, but not an arrangement where you live somewhere else. If the lease says that you cannot sublet at all, then you are not allowed to. Of course you can still ask the landlord to give permission, but if it is refused, there is nothing you can do.

More likely, you will be allowed to sublet if the landlord allows it (usually requiring 'prior written permission'). Whether or not the lease says so, the landlord may only refuse if it is reasonable to refuse. It is probably reasonable for the landlord to require personal references (eg from a previous landlord) and to reject any proposed subtenant who cannot provide them. The landlord must give an answer within a reasonable time, and if permission is refused, then written reasons must be given.

If the landlord refuses unreasonably or takes too long to respond, you have a right to compensation for loss, such as lost rent and advertising costs.

Alterations

You can usually decorate your flat as you wish, and carry out minor internal changes, but anything that involves structural work or that may have effects outside your flat, probably needs the landlord's permission first. For example: removing a wall (even non-loadbearing, as it may affect fire safety for other flats); exterior painting (your choice of colour and finish will change the overall appearance of the building).

The landlord need only be reasonable if the lease says so. If the landlord refuses your request, there may be nothing you can do, except for persuasion or moving. If you want to use a space that is not part of your flat, eg an unused loft or a flat roof, the landlord may want payment for that space. If you ask before you have done work, you may get a good price; if you wait until later, the landlord might charge you anything he or she sees fit.

Except in straightforward alterations, the landlord may want his own surveyor, architect or engineer to consider the proposed works. You will have to pay their fees, and they may have conditions that your contractors will have to keep to. There may be significant costs that you need to include in your budget for the work. In a large project, your architect or contractors may have to negotiate with the landlords and their professionals, which will mean further expense.

Administration charges

If you are asked to pay the landlord's fees or costs for:

- a permission
- information or documents
- late payment of rent or service charge
- breach of your lease (doing something that your lease prohibits)

these are administration charges. Since September 2003, only reasonable administration charges are payable. The Leasehold Valuation Tribunal can decide what is reasonable, whether you should pay, and can even change a lease if it fixes an unreasonable administration charge. You can dispute the amount of a charge even after paying it.

Flat management companies 7

Introduction

More and more flat owners are buying the freehold, or their landlord's leasehold reversion, of their building collectively. This can be through:

- voluntary sale by the landlord
- collective enfranchisement (see Chapter 3)
- the Right of First Refusal (see Chapter 4)
- compulsory acquisition (see Chapter 6).

Government statistics suggest that around 40 per cent of flat owners in England now also have a share in the freehold of their building. When the freehold or the lease of a block is bought, the flat owners will assume all the former landlord's rights and responsibilities. But how should the property be run?

Usually the first step is to form a flat management company whose role is to hold the legal interest in the property and, more practically, to manage the block. Often this company is, or was, the 'nominee purchaser' (under collective enfranchisement), or 'nominated person' (under the Right of First Refusal). Once a suitable flat management company has been formed, the owners need to consider such questions as organisation, meetings and managing agents.

Self-management by flat owners offers a number of advantages, including control over costs and maintenance, but it requires motivation, effort and no little skill to work properly. In the early 1990s, it was found that in self-managed blocks, complaints by long leaseholders were only about one-third and one-fifth as frequent than where the landlord was, respectively, an individual or a property company. Although flat management companies can be very effective, they are often poorly understood by many residents and some professionals. Success is highly dependent on the abilities and participation of company members. Experience and a number of studies have found that problems can be created by lack of interest, even apathy, among some flat owners, especially in larger blocks.

Commonhold associations

Commonhold associations own and manage the common parts and facilities of commonhold developments. A commonhold association is a private company limited by guarantee, whose membership is restricted to all the unit-holders within the development. In practical terms, therefore, many of the issues discussed in this chapter of importance to flat management companies will also be relevant to commonhold associations – with the exception of those relating to company formation.

There is not the space in this guide to examine all the aspects and implications of flat management companies. The Leasehold Advisory Service (LEASE) can help. So can the Federation of Private Residents' Associations (FPRA) – if you join (see Useful addresses, Chapter 12). Both also produce helpful publications.

This chapter looks at:

- Flat management companies.
- Running the company.
- Employing a managing agent.
- Potential problems.

Flat management companies

You need to decide early on how you want your building to be managed in the future. What sort of 'person' do you need to own the freehold or to hold the lease of the property? Some forms of flat management can be informal. For example, perhaps the simplest form of management structure is the case of a building converted into two or three flats. Responsibility for looking after the property can be shared equally between the owners and no other management structure may be needed. The freehold may be vested in one or more of the flat owners. This sort of arrangement would be only practical or sensible in very small blocks. In larger developments, more formal systems for self-management are appropriate. The most suitable vehicle is unquestionably a company. Alternative approaches are to establish a trust or another corporate body, such as an association.

Non-company alternatives for flat management

It is possible for two or more people to share ownership of a property, with the relationship between them governed by a 'trust'. A trust consists of a number of trustees regulated by a trust deed for the benefit of specific beneficiaries. In a joint-ownership trust, the trustees and beneficiaries are the same people. The trust deed would define each party's rights and obligations, including responsibility for common bills, maintenance and repairs. The 2000 Trustee Act governs trusts. A trust is not a corporate body: its income and liabilities are treated for tax and other purposes as belonging to the trustees. It is doubtful if a trust would be the most appropriate legal form for a building with more than six flats. A solicitor will be able to advise you about the mechanics of setting up a trust.

A non-company alternative is to set up an independent association which registers as an Industrial and Provident Society (IPS). Its rules have to be approved and as with a company, it has to file annual returns. The registration and regulation of Industrial and Provident Societies is the responsibility of the Financial Services Authority (FSA) from whom further information can be obtained. To form a society, normally at least seven people should be involved. Industrial and Provident Societies are not strictly companies and do not operate under company law, but must pool their resources on a self-help or co-operative basis. Members have limited liability for a society's debts. Individuals join or leave, but the corporate body lives on unless you collectively decide to dissolve it.

In almost all circumstances, especially in larger blocks, it is preferable to set up a limited company that acts as a kind of co-operative or collective vehicle for self-management. A limited company is a 'person' in its own right. This means it can own property and enter into contracts in its own name. It exists independently and separately from the flat owners. It allows the flat owners to be treated as a single body and, in addition, it provides a suitable degree of legal protection and a number of other safeguards. As shareholders, flat owners all have a say in running the limited company. Normally, the company's rules will state that shareholders who sell their flats must also transfer their share, or shares, to the new owner. This ensures that – at any given time – the limited company represents the interests of all the current flat owners.

Flat management companies set up by developers

Many developers of new blocks of flats establish flat management companies in advance of, or during, construction or conversion. Usually they transfer the freehold or a very long leasehold interest to the company. This is because they do not wish to have any management responsibilities once the flats are sold. As with commonhold associations, many of the issues discussed in this chapter will also be relevant to such companies – with the exception of those relating to formation.

Such companies can be known as tenants', residents', owners' or leaseholders' management companies, or simply as a 'flat management company'. Whatever its formal name, the role of a flat management company is to hold the ownership of, or legal interest in, the property and, more practically, to manage the block or building in which the flats are situated. They need to be distinguished from a tenants' association which, normally, does not have a legal interest in the property (see Tenants' associations, page 121).

Managing blocks of flats is a complex business. Buildings do not manage themselves. The skills required include:

- an understanding of leasehold law
- a knowledge of the statutory requirements
- compliance with the recognised codes of practice
- an understanding of buildings and their maintenance
- an awareness of health and safety and employment law and a wide range of other legal responsibilities.

Many flat owners – particularly in small blocks – carry out self-management perfectly well. However, self-management is too often reliant on a small group of volunteers prepared to give their time. This is not always ideal and is the reason why most large blocks of flats appoint a professional to manage the property on their behalf (see Managing agents later).

Management companies: limited by shares or by guarantee?

A company may either be limited by shares or by guarantee. Commonhold associations and Right to Manage companies have to be limited by guarantee. With a share company you buy a share for, say, £1, and as a shareholder you have a vote at shareholders' meetings. With a guarantee company you pay nothing immediately, but agree to pay a nominal sum (such as £1) if the company is wound up. Again, a member has the right to vote at meetings. The liability of shareholders or members for the debts of a company is limited, usually, to the value of their share or their guarantee. Both types have advantages depending on the circumstances and on the flat owners' wishes, although a company limited by guarantee is the recommended option. A solicitor will be able to advise you on the mechanics of setting up the most appropriate type of company.

The company's constitution (known as the Memorandum and Articles of Association) must be suitable. For example, membership must be restricted to flat owners. Normally this requirement is inserted in the memorandum, which would render it permanent and unalterable especially if the memorandum also prohibits any alteration of it. To ensure that all flat owners become members or shareholders of the company, the normal solution is to include in the lease a condition to that effect.

The company must also comply with the Companies Acts, including registration with Companies House, have at least one director and a secretary and send a copy of its full or abbreviated accounts annually to the Registrar of Companies. The company must have a registered office that may be a flat within the block or elsewhere (for example, at your managing agents or solicitors). If the company hires staff, such as a caretaker, it must comply with employment law. It must also comply with health and safety and all other relevant legislation. It is also a good idea to consider issues such as general safety, including fire precautions and security of the block.

By law, the company becomes the landlord and will be subject to all the legal obligations imposed on landlords under current legislation. These include the right of flat owners to:

- know how the service charge is made up
- inspect accounts and receipts
- challenge unreasonable service charges
- be consulted about major works.

Usually, only flat owners become directors of the management company. You may still need professional assistance, but co-operative management is likely to be better fostered if managing agents, auditors, etc are employed by the company, rather than joining its board. An appropriate number of directors, including a company secretary, are chosen from among the flat owners and are subject to periodic re-election.

Depending on the situation, the freehold or leasehold reversion to the leases of the individual flats is vested in the management company. Quite often, if it is a leasehold reversion, the leases are granted for 999 years – which to all intents and purposes makes it a 'freehold'. The freehold, or a lease of the common parts, is also usually granted to the management company. Once this has been done, the leases of the flat owners can be renewed. At the same time, the opportunity can be taken to correct any defects in, and/or vary the existing leases of the flats.

Running the company

Once a flat management company has been set up properly, there is usually no need ever to concern oneself with its structure or objectives again. There will though be regular administrative tasks associated with running a company. These include appointing directors, filing accounts with Companies House and holding an annual general meeting (AGM). Experience shows that problems rarely arise with these aspects of a company. Flat owners will be most concerned with the practical arrangements for running their block. In effect, they have assumed the full range of management responsibilities, including deciding and collecting service charges, and controlling and supervising all contracts covering the building. Managing a block of flats may seem a daunting prospect but many flat owners have managed it successfully. If there has been an effective tenants' or residents' association in the past, then you are likely to be familiar with much of what is involved. The chief difference will be that you will be commissioning work yourselves rather than checking on the actions of others.

Flat management advice

There are two excellent books about flat management. They are Cox's *Running a Flat Management Company* and Cumming's and Hickle's *How To Manage Your Own Block of Flats: A Flat Owners Guide to Taking and Maintaining Control*. For further details see Useful Publications, Chapter 11.

Once the practical day-to-day arrangements are in place, running the organisation should be straightforward. These include:

- electing the directors and appointing a secretary
- arranging the annual general meeting of the company
- organising further regular meetings, often on a quarterly basis
- operating a bank account and paying bills
- arranging insurance of the building
- preparing an annual budget
- fixing and arranging collection of service charges and, perhaps, ground rents
- deciding whether to engage a managing agent or not
- agreeing to maintenance contracts
- authorising and supervising major works

- dealing with employment of staff
- setting company policy
- preparing agendas for, and minutes of, meetings.

In practice, this work will depend on having sufficient flat owners who are prepared to do the work and to act as a director of the company. Flat owners need to be encouraged to participate in the management of the block. They need to report any defects in the property or their own flats, and to suggest improvements either to the property or the management of the block. It is possible for flat owners to decide to do some of the work previously carried out by paid contractors (for example, looking after the garden, decorating), although this should not be taken to extremes. In older blocks of flats, in particular, it is very important that timely maintenance and repairs are not overlooked. In most situations, you will require professional help before embarking on major works from a surveyor or architect. Major works also require you to obtain at least two tenders from builders.

Training in flat management skills

Participation in flat management is likely to be encouraged if training can be offered to members, particularly new members. Flat owners who have received training in appropriate skills are likely to be more confident and more competent. People could learn about keeping accounts and preparing budgets, becoming a company secretary, employment law and management skills. A number of organisations including colleges and adult education institutes run suitable courses and events. Many local authorities and housing associations offer training to their leaseholders and tenants. The Directory of Social Change (www.dsc.org.uk) and the National Council of Voluntary Organisations (www.ncvo.org.uk) run courses or have information about courses that are targeted at the voluntary sector.

The euphoria that can follow the acquisition of the freehold may soon disappear when the practical issues presented by self-management are realised. Self-management is not always a route to better management. Value for money services are a key benefit of self-management, but service charge arrears can be a problem, especially in larger blocks. There are reports of inadequate, even illegal, administration of flat management companies. It is important that these questions are fully considered by flat owners. The most common stumbling blocks are more easily avoided if forward planning is undertaken. The Federation of Private Residents Associations can help. Run by a voluntary committee of lawyers, property professionals and flat owners, the Federation is a non-profit making membership organisation which can advise flat owners before, during and after the purchase of the freehold (for its address, see Chapter 12).

Flat owners' experiences of self-management

A small case study of a number of self-managed blocks in 2004 found the following:

- Almost three-quarters of owners were satisfied, or very satisfied, with the flat management company.

- Around one half were involved with management in some – usually minor – way (ie reporting problems).

- Most felt more and better information before and after they bought their flat might encourage greater understanding and participation.

- Owners who sublet and young first time buyers were felt to lack sufficient motivation to get involved.

But:

- Almost one half were not happy with the service provided by their managing agent.

- A quarter did not even know their block was run by a flat management company.

- Almost one third of owners never attended meetings including the AGM.

Source: Paul Walentowicz, Unpublished research, 2005

Employing a managing agent

Property management is a complicated and professional business. Flat owners may not have the time or the skills that are required. Small blocks may be undemanding to manage, but if the building is large, it is usually preferable to employ a reputable managing agent to help with the day-to-day tasks of running a block. These tasks include:

- helping with budgets and accounts
- collecting service charges
- paying bills, including insurance premiums
- planning maintenance
- obtaining estimates for major works
- paying wages
- dealing with arrears and disputes.

Competent agents can reduce the time that some flat owners would otherwise have devoted to self-management and can prevent owners becoming involved in disputes with neighbours. The evidence is that flat management is better if a managing agent is employed. Most blocks of flats will already have a managing agent who used to act for the landlord. Unless you are very unhappy with their performance, it is better to retain them. You should choose a managing agent who is a member of a recognised professional body such as the Royal Institution of Chartered Surveyors (RICS) or the Association of Residential Managing Agents (ARMA). Both have professional codes of practice and are committed to promoting the highest standards of management.

A formal contract should be agreed between the company and the agent. If the contract is for more than one year, the formal consultation procedure must be carried out (see page 63). The agent should be bound by the appropriate professional code of conduct, and abide by the residential management code of practice published by the Royal Institution of Chartered Surveyors (see page 117).

Potential problems

It would not be true to pretend that a block that is resident-managed can be completely free of problems. Many of these will be similar to those that arose or might have arisen in the past. There can be a tension between a wish to keep service charges reasonable and the need for timely maintenance and repair. This can lead to the sort of problems illustrated in the two examples. It is important that the risk of this happening is recognised. A regular cycle of maintenance should be instituted and kept to. Appropriate and timely maintenance can postpone the need for future major repairs. It should be understood that repair or replacement works are done when needed and not put off. Unreasonable delay can result in the works costing far more than they would have done. There is a familiar stumbling block in blocks of flats – irrespective of whether they are run by a landlord or the owners – in getting agreement to carry out major improvements as distinct from repairs. Examples would be installing a lift, an entry phone system, replacing doors to an improved standard or modernising an older block in other ways. As buildings age, it is inevitable that they become increasingly obsolescent or out-of-date in many ways but, of course, this is ultimately reflected in the value of the flats. In reality, replacement or improvement of some parts of a property may have to wait until the work has to be done rather than because it would look nice or increase the value of the flats.

Examples

'In this block the priority was to keep the service charge down. It was done at the expense of the fabric of the block. That went on so long that there just became a backlog of things that needed to be done. Hence the (major refurbishment project), and people are now having to pay for it'.

Resident director, London mansion block of 108 flats

In order to keep the service charge low, the company's members decided that each leaseholder could do their own exterior work (!). Leaving such matters to individual leaseholders would thwart the purpose of collective management. It would be likely to lead to substandard work or the delaying of essential maintenance or repairs by some or perhaps most of the flat owners – with a consequent effect on the value of the flats.

Flat management company, Home Counties

It can be even more difficult to deal with 'difficult' or 'problem' owners. Handling service charge arrears might be comparatively straightforward, but grappling with the distress, inconvenience, quarrels and complaints caused by objectionable activities is never easy. Nuisance, or anti-social behaviour, includes excessive noise, inconsiderate residents or visitors, and residents who damage the property or who fail to act in an appropriate manner. Sometimes flat owners try to shift their problems onto the landlord, or try to use the landlord in personal vendettas, or stir up trouble with anonymous complaints. Unless it involves the block as a whole, it is often best to leave neighbours to sort out things themselves. Any landlord should be cautious about taking sides, and a flat management company should take particular care to be objective.

Local neighbourhood mediation services may be helpful in these situations. Excessive noise can lead to serious disputes. Local authority environmental health departments and the police have powers to act if noise nuisance is serious. Environmental health departments also have powers to take action against health hazards, such as overflowing cisterns and smoke from bonfires. Causing a nuisance, a disturbance, an inconvenience, or an annoyance is a breach of most leases. Landlords can ask the court to order the flat owner to comply with the lease, which may include the flat owner taking steps to prevent a family member, subtenant or visitor from behaving badly. Landlords can also claim damages. Ultimately, of course, the landlord can seek forfeiture in such cases. Note that most leases will allow one flat owner to force the landlord to take action against another who is causing a nuisance, but the first owner will have to pay the landlord's legal costs unless and until they can be recovered from the wrongdoer.

Nuisance and anti-social behaviour

We live in a small block of private, well-maintained flats (we own the freehold). Recently, one of the flats was bought as an 'investment opportunity' and the new owner is refurbishing the premises. For weeks, we have had to put up with debris dumped in the back garden. The owner has been asked to remove it but does not seem interested.

Daily Telegraph, 25 January 2003

A flat owner frequently played very loud music and kept people awake into the small hours. After a number of complaints from his near neighbours had been met with by, at first, unconcern and then hostility, the flat management company was asked to become involved. The local authority's Environmental Health Department was asked to monitor the property for noise offences and a letter was written by the managing agent to the owner reminding him of his responsibilities under the lease.

Flat management company, Birmingham, 1990s

Some of these problems are caused or exacerbated by the subletting of flats to tenants by owners. The Buy-to-Let boom has led in many areas to a huge increase in subletting: it is not uncommon to find blocks in which half of the residents are tenants. Most residential leases ban holiday-type and business lets, but permit subletting. Most leases also require that permission be obtained before a flat can be sold or let, but state that this should not be unreasonably withheld. Most mortgage deeds bar the creation of a tenancy without the lender's permission. Some insurance policies covering blocks of flats discourage or prohibit sublets to certain categories of higher risk tenant, such as those in receipt of social security benefits, or students. Subletting in such circumstances might render an insurance policy void or voidable: this could conceivably have a catastrophic impact on the owners. Even worse problems can be created if the sublets are short-term, with the tenants treating the property as if it was a hotel. Many absentee owners seem to lose interest in the property and its upkeep as long as they continue to receive their rental income. They are not prepared to become an active manager of their letting. Some mistakenly believe that it becomes the sole responsibility of the resident flat owners to look after the premises and to 'police' their tenant(s).

Example

A flat in a small self-managed block of six flats in Essex was sublet by the owner to a succession of short-term tenants for over ten years. During this time, the owner took no part in the management of the block, attended one residents' meeting, and when a problem arose with her tenants, referred the resident flat owners to her letting agent.

Recognising that this was a breach of her obligations under the lease, the management company decided to ask her to contribute an extra sum to its service charge account. She agreed to this request.

If a tenant behaves in an unacceptable manner, the absentee owner should be contacted and supplied with the details. Should further action be necessary, evidence of the problem will be needed. If the misbehaviour is serious and your requests that it cease are ignored, you might have to rely on the terms of the lease with respect to nuisance. Ultimately, you might have to seek forfeiture for breach of these terms.

Serious anti-social behaviour (for example, harassment, drug dealing, violence, prostitution, etc) is rare but should always be taken very seriously. The appropriate authorities (for example, the police) should usually be contacted. Much of this behaviour is criminal. If a flat owner is responsible, it is a breach of their lease as well. Local authorities now have a range of specific remedies, including Acceptable Behaviour Contracts (ABCs) and Anti-Social Behaviour Orders (ASBOs) to deal with significant incidents of unacceptable behaviour.

The Federation of Private Residents' Associations suggests that a set of House Rules for existing and new residents, including tenants, be drawn up and distributed. These could be used to inform people about the arrangements for running the block – for example, dealing with maintenance issues, reporting problems and dealing with complaints, the disposal and collection of rubbish, postal deliveries, etc. Owners and residents could also be reminded about their responsibilities – for example, to make service charge payments on time, to look after the property, to respect their neighbour's rights, not to make unacceptable noise, or cause a nuisance or disturbance, etc. Such rules could be updated regularly if you wanted to highlight a particular issue.

Some leases provide for rules to be introduced, others do not. Taking steps to discourage or prevent misbehaviour of any kind can be effective. You could consider employing a caretaker or having CCTV installed, although the cost of these would be reflected in service charges. Wide consultation and involvement is usually the best way to get flat owners and other residents to keep to the House Rules.

Indifference by flat owners towards the management of the block can also lead to other problems. Participating in the management of a resident-owned block is, of course, voluntary and you will find that many members rarely take part or, in some cases, never do so. Sometimes there are very good reasons, for example, health, family or work responsibilities. But sometimes there are not.

Example

'Some years ago we had a block of 104 flats ... and the freeholder was going to hand it all over you know. They set up a meeting (and) six people turned up so that's your apathy ... I've been to an AGM with those six committee members there, and one resident out of 104 flats. Why? Because they couldn't care less and a lot of them have sublet and are absentee landlords'.

Managing agent, large provincial town in the South-East

Lack of interest, even apathy, can – perhaps surprisingly – be prevalent even in situations where a large personal financial investment is at stake. One result of such indifference is the danger that unscrupulous individuals may come to dominate a management company and misuse their position for improper or even corrupt purposes. A managing agent might take advantage of such a situation and push up their fees, or become complacent about their management responsibilities. Low participation rates are likely to lead eventually to increased service charges. This would be because of an associated need to employ more professional help and assistance in the absence of greater resident participation. You might also point out that although participation is voluntary, so is buying a property in a resident-owned block.

It is difficult to suggest a permanent solution to this problem. If insufficient flat owners are prepared to help in running the block, a greater workload will fall on a smaller number of people. As long as they are prepared to carry on and do not abuse their authority, few difficulties should arise. But if not, the whole arrangement could break down with potentially serious consequences for the future of the block. Making participation more interesting and attractive might help. Directors and other meetings could be made less formal – perhaps with the exception of the annual general meeting – and official company business dealt with quickly and clearly. Greater opportunities could be provided for general discussion and debate. Providing refreshments might encourage attendance and encourage people to get to know each other. Such steps might help to boost participation and help to foster a community spirit.

Examples

One of the directors of a small flat management company in Essex failed to attend a single board or general meeting, including the annual meetings, for nearly three years without explanation and never found the time to even discuss issues informally with the other directors. Consequently, the workload fell disproportionately on the other two directors. On average, less than ten per cent of members attended quarterly meetings.

In a large block in central London, fewer than one in twenty flat owners attended the regular meetings and the company found it increasingly difficult to fill vacancies for directors. In another large London block with over 200 flats, over the years an average of 12 owners took an active part in its management.

To the extent that indifference is the result of a lack of information provided to new and existing flat owners, you could produce a Welcome Pack for new residents telling them about the management company and its role. Copies could also be provided to estate agents and to the managing agent to supply to a prospective purchaser's solicitor or conveyancer.

Resolving disputes   8

Introduction

Sometimes, disputes end up in court. Going to court is almost always expensive, time-consuming and worrying, and courts can often be unsettling and intimidating. Going to court should always be avoided if there are other ways of solving a problem or settling a dispute. You should first try to resolve a dispute by mutual agreement. If this is not successful, then you have a number of alternatives. This chapter briefly considers:

- What you should consider before you decide to fight a case.
- Leasehold Valuation Tribunals.
- Arbitration, mediation and other options.
- Going to court.

Before you decide to fight

If you are involved in a dispute with your landlord, there are some general points to consider:

- The landlord needs to do some things that you may not like, in order to comply with their duties under the lease and under the law. For example, the landlord needs to charge you for services and repairs. You may have to pay for services that do not benefit you or that you do not want.

- The relationship between flat owner and landlord is a long term one. It is usually better to resolve problems by discussion and negotiation than by legal procedures, which should only be used as a last resort.

- If you need to sell your flat, you will have to disclose existing disputes, and you may be asked about your relationship with your landlord generally. A dispute or a bad relationship may put a buyer off.

- You need to distinguish between minor and major issues. A particular item in dispute may only be worth a few pounds per flat, and is not worth a great deal of time and expense in argument. On the other hand, if you win the principle on something now, will it help you in the future? For example, an argument over a service charge item that will appear every year, or at regular intervals (eg if you are wrongly charged for lift repairs), may not be worth much this year, but over many years may be worth a lot of money.

- The costs of lawyers, surveyors and other professionals can be high. You should consider whether what is at stake is worth that cost.

- In most circumstances, your landlord can add to the service charge the costs of disputes, for example fees of managing agents and lawyers. You need to be sure that what you are arguing about is worthwhile. If you go to court, or to a Leasehold Valuation Tribunal, you may be able to make the landlord pay for their own costs, but you cannot count on such an outcome.

- Your flat is a valuable asset and probably the most valuable thing you own. You need to make sure that you do not put the asset at risk. You should not refuse or fail to pay ground rent, and you should not breach the terms of the lease. If you are uncertain as to your rights, get advice from a solicitor or the Citizens Advice Bureau (CAB) or similar advice service.

- Leases are complicated legal documents that are not written in plain English. It can be difficult to find relevant clauses, and easy to misunderstand their provisions. If there is an argument about what your lease means, you should almost always get advice from a solicitor or the Citizens Advice Bureau.

- Disputes about your lease may be time-consuming, tiring and stressful. Do you have the resources for a fight?
- Waiting times for getting to court or tribunal can be many months.
- Where possible, you should discuss your concerns with other flat owners. If the majority of flat owners make a stand, the landlord is more likely to listen than if a small minority try to do so. Disputes about leases can take time and money, and the burden is best spread. It is usually best if all the flat owners act together, preferably through a recognised tenants' association.

Leasehold Valuation Tribunals

Many disputes between flat owners and their landlords can now be dealt with by a Leasehold Valuation Tribunal (LVT) rather than a court. The LVT can:

- decide the price to be paid to enfranchise (buy the freehold) or extend the lease
- vary an estate management scheme
- adjudicate in disputes about the Right of First Refusal procedure and compulsory acquisition of the landlord's interest
- decide disputes about service charges and administration charges, and about the landlord's choice of insurer
- deal with landlords' applications for dispensation of service charge consultation requirements; flat owners' applications on the right to manage and appointment of managers; and applications for variation of leases and estate charges.

The LVT should be the last resort for any dispute that it is able to deal with. If a case is started in court, which should have been brought in the LVT, or if during a court case issues are raised that should be dealt with by the LVT, the court will usually halt the court case and refer it to the LVT. The LVT cannot deal with disputes that are outside its powers.

The paperwork is simpler and more informal in the LVT than at court. There are still forms to be used and procedures to be followed, and you should get professional advice or information from the Residential Property Tribunal Service (RPTS) before applying and as your application progresses. There is usually an application fee, which may be remitted for those in receipt of most means-tested social security benefits, or for those who have a civil legal aid certificate for cases transferred from a court. The LVT has the discretion to require any party to the proceedings to reimburse either part or all of the fee to the applicant. LVT hearings are more informal than court hearings, and it is not necessary, although it is often advisable, to be represented by a solicitor or other professional. There will usually be three members of the LVT, which may include lawyers, surveyors and/or people without relevant qualifications. The decision of the LVT is final, although there is a limited right of appeal to the Lands Tribunal (LT). Apart from the application fee, the LVT cannot make the losing side pay the winning side's legal costs.

The landlord can usually add legal costs to the service charge. This would mean that the costs would be payable by all of the flat owners and not just those who went to the LVT. However, if the LVT thinks this would be unfair (for example where the flat owners won on all or most points), the LVT can decide that the landlord should not add legal costs to the service charge.

Arbitration, mediation and other options

You should always consider options other than going to court or the LVT. Other methods may be cheaper and/or quicker, and may be less damaging to the relationship between you and your landlord. You should consider the following:

Arbitration

Arbitration is like a court or tribunal, but an arbitrator, who is chosen and paid by the parties to the dispute, makes the decision. Often a lease will say that arbitration must be used for certain disputes (eg about service charges), which may well mean that the court and LVT cannot decide. Such a lease will usually explain how an arbitrator should be chosen, often a surveyor chosen by the President of the Royal Institution of Chartered Surveyors (RICS). If the lease does not require arbitration, the parties to a dispute can still agree to go to arbitration if they want to. In most cases, the LVT is better than arbitration, but arbitration might be a good choice in a case where the LVT has no power to decide and the parties do not want to go to court, or in a case where a quick decision is needed (eg to allow a sale to proceed).

The procedure is up to the arbitrator and to the parties to the dispute. Professional advice is usually advisable. An arbitrator's decision, once made, is binding. There are limited rights of appeal.

Complaints procedures

All councils, housing associations and many other large landlords have a complaints procedure, which is suitable for resolving some leasehold disputes. The complaints procedure may be particularly useful where you feel that you are being dealt with unfairly, or the landlord is breaking their own rules, but it is unlikely to be useful where there is a major dispute. The Local Government Ombudsman (LGO) and Housing Ombudsman Service (HOS) provide a further service if local authorities and housing associations fail to deal with your complaint properly, but they do not generally deal with the detail of the underlying dispute. You should get advice from a Citizens Advice Bureau or other adviser before spending time and energy on applying to an ombudsman.

Where there is a managing agent who is a member of a professional organisation (eg RICS or ARMA, see Chapter 12), that organisation will have a complaints procedure. Check that your dispute is covered by the procedure before trying to use it. A professional organisation will be concerned about dishonesty or a breach of its rules, but is unlikely to be interested in specific service charge items.

Mediation

Mediation is a form of negotiation where a neutral mediator helps to bring about an agreement, usually during a day or half day session. There is only a binding outcome if agreement can be reached, and that is only likely if everyone involved is willing to consider a reasonable compromise. Your landlord may already be a member of a mediation scheme. If not, there are a number of schemes available: one is provided by the Leasehold Advisory Service (LEASE) (see Chapter 12).

The parties to the dispute usually pay the mediator's fee, although many schemes are subsidised and have limited fees. For example, the Leasehold Advisory Service scheme costs £100 per party, which makes it cheaper than most other dispute resolution options. Mediation is a good option where both sides would like to resolve the dispute and are willing to compromise to achieve that.

Third party determination

It may be helpful to allow a neutral third party to have the final say. This may be particularly useful where the amount in dispute is quite small. A surveyor could be asked to value work done. Make sure that what is being agreed is decided in advance (eg is the third party simply advising or making a binding decision?) and that the agreement is recorded in writing.

Negotiation

Some leasehold disputes continue for months or years. As long as progress is being made, this is not necessarily a bad thing, but you should consider at regular intervals whether some other procedure could be used.

Your lease may specify a particular method of resolving disputes. Some of these are binding. For example, if your lease says that an arbitrator must determine service charge disputes if not agreed, that will probably prevent an application to the LVT or court, but will not prevent negotiation or mediation. Your lease may require a period of negotiation, or for mediation to take place, and this will usually require you and your landlord to try to find a settlement using the procedure indicated. The lease cannot force you to agree, but can provide a method by which agreement may be reached.

Going to court

Sometimes, however, going to court is the only way that a flat owner can enforce their rights, for example, to make their landlord carry out repairs. In such cases, it may be necessary to go to court to get an order to compel the landlord to carry out the repairs. On the other hand, if a landlord threatens legal proceedings and the flat owners have obtained legal advice that they have a strong defence, there may be no way of avoiding a court hearing.

The usual court in England and Wales for civil action about most leasehold issues is the county court. In those rare cases where criminal proceedings are necessary, these usually start in the magistrates court. You can find the address of the court from the Court Service, or from a local directory (but check with the court that it is the right one – sometimes, especially in London, the nearest court is not necessarily the right court).

If you are bringing a case in the county court ('suing'), you are called the 'claimant', and if you are defending a claim you are called the 'defendant'. The case is started by a 'claim form'. Centuries of baffling legal terminology have been laid to rest in recent years, and terms like 'plaintiffs' and 'writ' are no longer used. If a case is defended, it will be allocated to one of three tracks: small claims (generally claims up to £5,000), fast track (£5,000-15,000) and multi-track (£15,000+). You can probably deal with a case yourself in the small track, perhaps with occasional advice, but you are likely to need professional advice in the fast track and you will need it for multi-track.

If you are considering going to court:

- You should always get professional advice. You can get initial advice from housing advice centres, Citizens' Advice Bureaux and similar consumer advice bodies. They are usually not able to give you expert advice on a leasehold problem but should be able to put you in touch with someone, probably a solicitor, who can. The Leasehold Advisory Service can provide advice by telephone, by letter, or in person at its office but it cannot act directly for you, offer long-term supportive casework, or provide any service usually facilitated by a solicitor or surveyor (its address is given in Chapter 12). If court proceedings are approaching, your best bet is to seek the help of a solicitor. Ideally, the solicitor should be one who specialises in disputes involving flat owners and their landlords.

- You may be eligible for civil legal aid, which means that your solicitor can represent you free of charge, or you will have to pay a reduced contribution. Civil legal aid can be available for most court proceedings and Lands Tribunal hearings. Information about legal aid is available from the Legal Services Commission (LSC). There is a means test, and you will only qualify if you have a low income and few savings. As well as the means test, there is a merits test, in which you need to show that your case justifies the legal costs involved. You need a sufficiently large dispute and a good chance of winning. It is difficult to get legal aid for a dispute about service charges, as the amount at stake is generally relatively small.
  If going to court will benefit other people, for example, if you are seeking an order requiring your landlord to repair the roof of a block containing several other flats, then you might be refused legal aid, or have to pay an increased contribution on the assumption that the other flat owners will help with the legal costs. If you win your case and you get or keep money with the help of legal aid, you may be asked to put it towards your solicitor's bill, and in some cases the Legal Services Commission will put a charge (like a mortgage, but payable on sale of the property) on your home for the amount of the bill.

- Many solicitors will give you a free or fixed price interview or advice.

- If you do not qualify for legal aid and cannot afford the full cost of going to court, some lawyers will take up your case on a 'no-win-no-fee' basis. Your case has to be a strong one, and if you win you may have to pay extra costs as well as any costs recovered from the landlord.

- If you receive a claim form from your landlord, you must act very quickly. In some cases, you must file a defence within two weeks and, if you do not do so in time, you may be prevented from defending the case.

- If you lose a court case, it is probable that you will have to pay your landlord's legal fees as well as your own. Such costs may run to thousands of pounds. On the other hand, if you win, you stand a good chance of getting back most of your legal costs. You should remember that your potential liability for costs starts from the moment that a claim form is issued.

- If you think that you may become involved in going to court, keep all papers which may be useful, and make notes immediately anything relevant happens (for example, a conversation with the managing agent, or the date when you noticed that something needed repairing). If you make notes immediately after each incident, you will be able to use them to remind yourself when you are giving evidence in court.

Glossary

9

---

arbitration
Settling a dispute by using an arbitrator or independent referee. It avoids using the courts or a Leasehold Valuation Tribunal.

assignment
The transfer of a property right or lease from one person to another.

assured tenancy
A form of private tenancy introduced by the 1988 Housing Act. Assured tenants have limited security of tenure and pay a market level of rent. Assured shorthold tenancies are now the 'default' or standard form of private tenancy.

auditor
Someone, usually an accountant, responsible for certifying that the accounts of an organisation are a correct and true representation of its financial affairs.

breach
When a term of a lease is broken.

civil law
That part of the law that confers rights and imposes duties on individuals and others. Most activities involving the leasehold system are subject to the civil law. Sometimes a breach of the civil law can result in criminal sanctions.

collective enfranchisement
The process by which flat owners can together acquire the freehold of their block.

commonhold

A type of ownership in England and Wales for interdependent properties such as blocks of flats, shops and offices. Each flat is owned on a freehold basis, with freehold ownership and management of the common parts and facilities undertaken by the commonhold association of which all flat owners are members.

common law

That part of the law in England and Wales that is derived from custom and judicial precedent rather than from statutes or Acts of Parliament.

company

A corporate body registered under the Companies Acts. Companies are either owned by their shareholders, or have members who guarantee to pay the debts of the company up to a limited amount.

Communities and Local Government (CLG)

Formerly known as the Department for Communities and Local Government which succeeded the Office of the Deputy Prime Minister (ODPM) in May 2006. It is responsible for housing policy.

contract

A legally binding agreement.

County Court

Deals with the great majority of civil cases in England and Wales, including some leasehold issues. Leasehold Valuation Tribunals now deal with very many leasehold disputes, not county courts.

covenants

Legally binding obligations and responsibilities. Covenants cover undertakings between landlord and flat owner under which each is legally bound to do certain things. For example, a landlord covenants to provide certain services, while a flat owner covenants to pay a service charge. Covenants may be expressed (ie set out in a lease) or implied. Covenants are 'promises' that can be enforced by the courts, even if someone does not realise they have made them.

criminal law
That part of the law concerned with the punishment of offenders.

deed
A document that creates, varies or transfers legal rights or obligations. For example, a document which transfers ownership of property from one person to another.

demised premises
Property which is the subject matter of a lease.

Department for Constitutional Affairs (DCA)
The DCA is responsible for commonhold matters.

determine
To end or decide.

easement
The legal right over another's land.

enfranchisement
The legal right of flat owners to collectively buy the freehold of their block.

extension
The right of most flat owners to seek a new lease.

forfeiture
A legal process by which a landlord can bring a lease to an early end and regain possession of their property because the lease conditions have not been met. Much limited by statute law.

freehold
A form of tenure giving outright ownership of land for all time.

grant
Transferring the ownership of property.

ground rent
A fee – usually small – paid periodically by a flat owner to the landlord as a condition of their lease. See also 'peppercorn rent'.

implied term
Read into a lease rather than being spelled out in it.

landlord
The owner of a property who grants a lease or sublease of the property. See 'lessor'.

The Land Registry
The government agency which registers title to land in England and Wales.

The Lands Tribunal
Appeals against a decision of a Leasehold Valuation Tribunal are made to the Lands Tribunal.

lease
A document which creates the leasehold, setting out all the rights and obligations of the landlord and the flat owner or leaseholder. It gives the flat owner sole use of the property for an agreed period of time.

leasehold
A form of tenure which gives the flat owner possession of the property for a long period of time, which is clearly defined in the lease.

Leasehold Valuation Tribunal
An independent and impartial body who are appointed to make decisions on various types of dispute relating to residential leasehold property. There are five regional offices in England. Part of the Residential Property Tribunal Service (RPTS).

lessee
The person to whom a lease was originally granted or, more commonly, the present leaseholder. In this guide, the term 'flat owner' is used to describe a lessee, tenant or leaseholder who owns, or is buying, their flat.

lessor
The person who originally granted a lease; also, the present landlord.

management audit
The right of flat owners to carry out a management audit to satisfy themselves that the landlord is administering service charges effectively and efficiently.

managing agent
An individual or firm which manages a block of flats on behalf of the owner. Many managing agents are surveyors.

marriage value
In collective enfranchisement, marriage value is the extra value brought about by the freehold and leasehold interests being brought together. These interests are often worth more together than apart.

mediation
A way of settling disputes. Mediation is an approach to negotiation in which an independent mediator helps the disputing parties reach agreement, usually during a day or half-day session.

Office of the Deputy Prime Minister (ODPM)
The government department responsible for housing policy until May 2006. See also *Communities and Local Government (CLG).*

peppercorn rent
A peppercorn rent means a rent of no value.

premium
The capital sum or purchase price paid for a long lease.

Protection from Eviction Act
A law making it a criminal offence for a landlord to evict a residential tenant without first getting a court order. A tenant who has been illegally evicted can also claim damages.

qualifying tenant
A person who qualifies for enfranchisement, a lease extension, the Right to Manage (RTM) and/or the Right of First Refusal.

register
In the case of a property with a registered title, the record for that property kept at the Land Registry.

Rent Assessment Committee
An independent local tribunal with a variety of functions relating to private sector rents. Part of the Residential Property Tribunal Service (RPTS).

Rent Assessment Panel
Has jurisdiction over the recognition of tenants' associations. Part of the Residential Property Tribunal Service.

reserve fund
A fund to hold money collected through service charges to meet the costs of future major works – it can be for a specific matter or for major repairs generally.

Residential Property Tribunal Service
The umbrella organisation for Rent Assessment Panels (RAPs), Rent Assessment Committees (RACs) and Leasehold Valuation Tribunals (LVTs).

reversion
A landlord's right to possession of a flat when the lease ends.

Right of First Refusal
The right of tenants of flats, including flat owners, to collectively buy their building if their landlord wishes to dispose of it.

Right to Buy
The right of tenants of social landlords (usually local authorities) to buy the freehold or the leasehold of their house or flat.

Right to Manage (Private sector)
The right of flat owners to collectively manage their building or block. This right was introduced in the 2002 Commonhold and Leasehold Reform Act.

Right to Manage (Public sector)
A similar right for council tenants and leaseholders, including flat owners, exercised under different legislation than that applying to the private sector.

section 20 notice
A notice served under s20 of the 1985 Landlord and Tenant Act in respect of proposed major works.

security of tenure
The right to remain in possession after the original contract has expired.

service charge
The charge made to a flat owner for the provision of services under the lease.

sinking fund
See reserve fund.

statute law
Acts of Parliament.

subletting

A subletting occurs when the owner of a lease grants a tenancy or a lease – with a shorter term – of the property.

superior landlord

Someone with a higher interest than the flat owner's immediate landlord. If A, a freeholder, grants a 999 year lease to B and B then grants a 99 year lease to C, a flat owner, the superior landlord is A. A is the landlord of B. B is the landlord of C.

tenant

The person to whom a lease is granted. In this guide, the term 'flat owner' is used to describe a tenant who owns or is buying their flat.

tenure

How land is legally held by the owner (for example, freehold or leasehold).

term

This means either the length of a lease (in years) or a condition contained in a lease.

title

Ownership of a property.

title deeds

Documents which prove who owns a property and under what terms.

valuer

A professional trained in property valuation. Most valuers are surveyors.

variation

Refers to changing the terms of a lease.

Main Acts of Parliament

10

Landlord and Tenant Act 1985

- Gives flat owners rights in relation to service charges.
- Right to be consulted about major works.
- Right to information about, and to challenge, service charges.
- Rights relating to insurance.
- Right to have a recognised tenants' association.
- Right to be consulted about managing agents.

Landlord and Tenant Act 1987

- Gives qualifying tenants, including flat owners, the Right of First Refusal – the right to buy their landlord's interest if he wants to sell.
- Right to seek the appointment of a manager.
- Rights to compulsory purchase of a landlord's interest.
- Requires service charges to be held in a separate account and on trust.
- Right to seek variation of their leases.

Local Government and Housing Act 1989 (Schedule 10)

- Gives most flat owners the right to remain as a renting tenant at the end of their lease.

Leasehold Reform, Housing and Urban Development Act 1993

- Gives most flat owners the collective right to buy their freehold.
- Gives most flat owners the individual right to extend their lease.

- Right to a management audit.
- Gives the Secretary of State and the National Assembly of Wales the power to approve management codes of practice.
- Gives landlord's of leasehold flats the right to apply for an estate management scheme.

Housing Act 1996

- Makes it easier to challenge unreasonable service charges.
- Restricts a landlord's right to forfeit if an item or items of service charges are disputed.
- Strengthens the Right of First Refusal.
- Extends the right of flat owners to buy the freehold of their building.
- Gives jurisdiction to Leasehold Valuation Tribunals to determine service charge disputes and applications for the appointment of a manager.

Commonhold and Leasehold Reform Act 2002

- Introduces the commonhold scheme for the ownership of flats and other interdependent units.
- Further improves the right of flat owners to buy the freehold of their building.
- Widens the right to seek the appointment of a new manager.
- Widens the grounds under which a lease can be varied.
- Introduces the Right to Manage.
- Improves the right to be consulted about service charges (qualifying works and long term agreements).
- Improves rights in relation to ground rents and forfeiture.
- Widens the jurisdiction of Leasehold Valuation Tribunals to determine the liability to pay service charges, the reasonableness of administration charges and variation of leases.

Useful publications

11

Companies House

Flat Management Companies (GBA9), **February 2005**

Lengthy advice aimed at smaller flat management companies.
Covers Right to Manage companies and commonhold
associations. Available on the Companies House website.

Communities and Local Government (CLG)

Residential Long Leaseholders: a guide to your rights and responsibilities **(July 2005)**

Almost 140 pages of advice from the Government. Available on
the CLG website, or by post from the address below.

Right to Manage Guidance for Tenant Management Organisations **(July 2005)**

The guidance consists of a pack of eight volumes. Although
aimed at local authority tenants and leaseholders, private sector
flat owners might find one or two of the volumes interesting and
helpful. The pack contains:

- The New Modular Management Agreement for TMOs.
- A Guidance on Schedules.
- Calculating Allowances for TMOs.
- Getting Started – Guidance on set up costs for TMOs.
- The Model Code of Governance for TMOs and guidance on
  confidentiality.

- The Guide to the Right to Manage.
- Preparing to Manage.
- Learning to Manage.

These can be read on or downloaded from the website. Printed copies can be obtained individually or as a set.

Communities and Local Government
CLG Publications
PO Box No 236
Wetherby LS23 7NB

Tel: 0870 1226 236   Fax: 0870 1226 237
Email: communities@twoten.com
Website: www.communities.gov.uk

The Department for Constitutional Affairs (DCA)

Model commonhold documents

Memorandum of Association.

Articles of Association.

Commonhold Community Statement.

Forms (Schedule 4 of the Commonhold Regulations).

DCA commonhold guidance

Non-Statutory Guidance on the Commonhold Regulations 2004.

Guidance on the drafting of a Commonhold Community Statement.

Commonhold – Frequently Asked Questions.

Available on the DCA website: www.dca.gov.uk

The Federation of Private Residents' Associations (FPRA)

Information Pack

A guide to setting up a residents' association.

Variation of Leases.

A checklist of conditions to consider when redrafting a lease after freehold purchase.

Summary of Rights

A summary of rights conferred by statute on residential tenants and leaseholders.

Rights and Duties of Leaseholders and Directors

A flow chart summarising rights and responsibilities.

FPRA also produces a quarterly newsletter for its members.

The Land Registry

Guide to commonhold

Guidance on the procedure for registration of a commonhold. The Land Registry also provides a range of forms relevant to commonhold and leasehold. Available on the Land Registry website: www.landreg.gov.uk

The Leasehold Advisory Service (LEASE)

Application to the Leasehold Valuation Tribunal

Appointing a Managing Agent – The need, selection and working with them

Appointment of a Surveyor/Management Audits

Collective Enfranchisement – Getting started

Collective Enfranchisement – Valuation

Commonhold

Lease Extension – Getting started

Lease Extension – Valuation

Lease Mediation Service

Leasehold Retirement Housing

Living in Leasehold Flats – A guide to how it works

Participation Agreements

Right of First Refusal

Right to Manage

Section 20 Consultation (Council and Other Public Sector Landlords)

Section 20 Consultation

Security of Tenure When The Lease Runs Out

Service Charges, Ground Rent and Forfeiture

Available on the LEASE website: www.lease-advice.org.uk

The Legal Action Group (LAG)

Francis Davey and Justin Bates, *Leasehold Disputes: a guide to Leasehold Valuation Tribunals*, 2004

Order from:
Legal Action Group
242 Pentonville Road, London N1 9UN
Tel: 020 7833 7424   Fax: 020 7837 6094
Email: books@lag.org.uk
Website: www.lag.org.uk

The Residential Property Tribunal Service (RPTS)

Leasehold Valuation Tribunals – Leasehold Service Charges

Leasehold Valuation Tribunals – Leasehold Enfranchisement

Leasehold Valuation Tribunals – Guidance on Procedure

Tenants' Associations

RPTS also supplies appropriate forms for leasehold disputes.
Available on the RPTS website: www.rpts.gov.uk

The Royal Institution of Chartered Surveyors (RICS)

Service Charge Residential Management Code, 1997

The Code provides best practice advice for the management of residential property. An addendum was added in 2005. An up-to-date version of the Code is expected during 2007.

In addition a number of other organisations publish books which may be of interest. Please note that some of these books are aimed at lawyers, surveyors, managing agents, other professionals and people with a specialist knowledge in the field.

D. Clarke, *Commonhold: The New Law*, Jordan, 2002.

N. G. Cox, *Running a Flat Management Company*, 4th edition, Jordan, 2004.

J. Cumming and R. Hickle, *How To Manage Your Own Block of Flats: A Flat Owners Guide to Taking and Maintaining Control,* 2nd edition, College of Estate Management, 2004.

G. Fetherstonhaugh, S. Peters and M. Sefton, *Commonhold*, Oxford University Press, 2004.

B. Jones, *Right to Manage and Service Charges*, EG Books, 2003.

B. Jones, *Enforcing Covenants*, EG Books, 2006.

P. Robinson, *Leasehold Management: A Good Practice Guide*, Chartered Institute of Housing, the National Housing Federation and the Housing Corporation, 2004.

C. Ward, *Residential Leaseholders Handbook*, EG Books, 2006.

Useful addresses 12

Information and advice (government departments)

Communities and Local Government (CLG)
Leasehold Reform Team
Zone 2/H10
Eland House
Bressenden Place
London SW1E 5DU

Tel: 020 7944 4287
Website: www.communities.gov.uk

(The CLG was formerly known as Department for Communities and Local Government which succeeded the Office of the Deputy Prime Minister (ODPM) in May 2006).

The Welsh Assembly Government
Housing Directorate
Private Rented & Rent Officer Service Branch
Ground Floor
Cathays Park
Cardiff CF10 3NQ

Tel: 029 2082 3025
Website: www.wales.gov.uk

The Department for Constitutional Affairs (DCA)
Selborne House
54 Victoria Street
London SW1E 6QW

Tel: 020 7210 8614
Website: www.dca.gov.uk

Government offices cannot give advice on individual cases, but may be able to answer general enquiries and provide information about commonhold and the leasehold system.

Information and advice (independent)

The Federation of Private Residents' Associations (FPRA)
59 Mile End Road
Colchester CO4 5BU

Tel: 0871 200 3324
Fax: 01206 851 616

Email: info@fpra.org.uk
Website: www.fpra.org.uk

FPRA is a voluntary organisation for flat management companies. It offers support and a range of services to its members. These include publications, legal and other advice. Has a helpful website with useful links.

The Leasehold Advisory Service (LEASE)
31 Worship Street
London EC2A 2DX

Tel: 020 7374 5380
Fax: 020 7374 5373

Email: info@lease-advice.org
Website: www.lease-advice.org.uk

LEASE is an independent advice agency, funded by the Government, to give free initial advice on the law affecting residential long leasehold property and commonhold. Produces a wide range of detailed publications. LEASE also offers a mediation service.

Other organisations

The Association of Residential Managing Agents (ARMA)
178 Battersea Park Road
London SW11 4ND

Tel: 020 7978 2607
Fax: 020 7498 6153

Email: info@arma.org.uk
Website: www.arma.org.uk

ARMA maintains a list of its members. Its code of practice and other publications are downloadable from its website. ARMA set up the Institute of Residential Property Management (IRPM) in 2002 to promote education in property management.

The Association of Retirement Housing Managers (ARHM)
Southbank House
Black Prince Road
London SE1 7SJ

Tel: 020 7463 0660
Fax: 020 7463 0661

Email: enquiries@arhm.org
Website: www.arhm.org

Companies House
Main Office
Companies House
Crown Way
Maindy
Cardiff CF14 3UZ

London
Companies House Executive Agency
21 Bloomsbury Street
London WC1B 3XD

Companies House Contact Centre
Tel: 0870 333 3636

Email: enquiries@companies-house.gov.uk

Companies House deals with the registration and regulation of companies. Its website is www.companieshouse.gov.uk

The Council of Mortgage Lenders (CML)
3 Savile Row
London W1S 3PB

Tel: 020 7437 0075
Fax: 020 7434 3791

Website: www.cml.org.uk

CML is the representative group for mortgage lenders in the UK.

The Financial Services Authority (FSA)
25 The North Colonnade
Canary Wharf
London E14 5HS

Tel: 020 7066 1000
Fax: 020 7066 1099

Website: www.fsa.gov.uk

The registration and regulation of mutual societies including friendly societies is now the responsibility of the FSA.

Her Majesty's Courts Service
Customer Service Unit
5th Floor
Clive House
Petty France
London SW1H 9HD

Tel: 020 7189 2000 or 0845 456 8770
Fax: 020 7189 2732

Website: www.hmcourts-service.gov.uk

HM Courts Service is an executive agency of the Department for Constitutional Affairs (DCA). Its website includes details about all the Service's courts and how to find them, as well as information about procedures and processes, forms and guidance.

The Land Registry (Head Office)
Lincoln's Inn Fields
Chancery Lane
London WC2A 3PH

Tel: 020 7917 8888
Fax: 020 7955 0110

Website: www.landreg.gov.uk

or

Wales Office
Tel: 01792 355000
Fax: 01792 355055

The Land Registry registers title to land in England and Wales and records sales and mortgages involving registered land. It maintains a network of local offices in England, and publishes a series of guides and official forms, including those for commonhold.

The Lands Tribunal
By post
The Lands Tribunal
Procession House
55 Ludgate Hill
London EC4M 7JW

Tel: 020 7029 9780
Fax: 020 7029 9781

Website: www.landstribunal.gov.uk

The Lands Tribunal is the body to whom an appeal can be made against a decision of a Leasehold Valuation Tribunal.

The Law Centres Federation (LCF)
Duchess House
18-19 Warren Street
London W1T 5LR

Tel: 020 7387 8570
Fax: 020 7387 8368

Email: info@lawcentres.org.uk
Website: www.lawcentres.org.uk

The LCF is the voice of Law Centres. They provide free
independent legal advice and representation to disadvantaged
members of society. You can find a centre near you, via the
website above.

The Legal Services Commission (Head Office)
85 Gray's Inn Road
London WC1X 8TX

Tel: 020 7759 0000

Website: www.legalservices.gov.uk

The Legal Services Commission looks after legal aid in England
and Wales. Through its Community Legal Service it funds a
network of solicitors, Citizens' Advice Bureaux and other advice
providers. Help varies from information leaflets to taking cases to
court where necessary.

The National Association of Citizens Advice Bureaux
Myddelton House
115-123 Pentonville Road
London N1 9LZ

Tel: 020 7833 2181
Fax: 020 7833 4371

Website: www.citizensadvice.org.uk

Citizens Advice provides support and services to its individual Bureaux. It does not give advice to the public; that is the job of local Bureaux. You can find your local Bureaux via the website.

National Federation of Tenant Management Organisations (NFTMO)

c/o Burrowes Street TMC
Resource Centre
Burrowes Street
Walsall WS2 8NN

Tel: 01704 227053
Website: www.nftmo.com

NFTMO provides advice, support and guidance to public sector tenant management organisations.

The National Archives

The National Archives handles a great deal of information, including that previously dealt with by Her Majesty's Stationery Office (HMSO) and Office of Public Sector Information (OPSI). Its website holds all UK legislation, including Regulations and Orders dating from about 1988 onwards. Details are available from www.direct.gov.uk

The Residential Property Tribunal Service (RPTS)

10 Alfred Place
London WC1E 7LR

Tel: 020 7446 7751 (Helpline: 0845 600 3178)
Fax: 020 7580 5684

Website: www.rpts.gov.uk

The RTPS is the umbrella organisation for Rent Assessment Panels, Rent Assessment Committees and Leasehold Valuation Tribunals.

The Royal Institution of Chartered Surveyors (RICS)
RICS Contact Centre
Surveyor Court
Westwood Way
Coventry CV4 8JE

Tel: 0870 333 1600
Fax: 020 7334 3811

Email: contactrics@rics.org
Website: www.rics.org

RICS is the professional association for surveyors and valuers.

Shelter
88 Old Street
London EC1V 9HU

Helpline: 0808 800 4444 (8am to midnight, seven days a week)

Website: www.shelter.org.uk

Shelter helps homeless and badly-housed people through its
Housing Aid Centres and practical projects, and via its free
housing advice helpline, the internet and email.

The Stationery Office (TSO)
TSO Orders/Post Cash Dept
PO Box 29
Norwich NR3 1GN

Tel: 0870 600 5522
Fax: 0870 600 5533

Email: customer.services@tso.co.uk
Website: www.tso.co.uk

Prints and sells parliamentary and government publications.

Tenant Participation Advisory Service (TPAS)
5th Floor
Trafford House
Chester Road
Manchester M32 0RS

Tel: 0161 868 3500
Fax: 0161 877 6256

Email: info@tpas.org.uk
Website: www.tpas.org.uk

TPAS England is a leading tenant participation organisation
for social housing tenants and leaseholders. It offers a range
of services, including a helpline, an information service,
conferences and training programmes.

Leasehold Valuation Tribunals 13

In England (Part of the Residential Property Tribunal Service)

London
10 Alfred Place, London WC1E 7LR
Tel: 020 7446 7700
Fax: 020 7637 1250/020 7637 9789

Eastern
Great Eastern House, Tenison Road, Cambridge CB1 2TR
Tel: 0845 100 2616
Fax: 01223 505116

Midlands
2nd Floor, East Wing, Ladywood House,
45/46 Stephenson Street, Birmingham B2 4UZ
Tel: 0845 100 2615
Fax: 0121 643 7605

Northern
20th Floor, Sunley Tower, Piccadilly Plaza, Manchester M1 4BE
Tel: 0845 100 2614
Fax: 0161 237 3656

Southern
1st Floor, Midland House, 1 Market Avenue, Chichester PO19 1PJ
Tel: 0845 100 2617
Fax: 01243 779389

In Wales (sponsored by the Welsh Assembly Government)

1st Floor, West Wing, Southgate House, Wood Street,
Cardiff CF1 1EW
Tel: 029 209 22 777
Fax: 029 202 36 146

Index